Slices Make A Loaf

Your manual for making millions fast by dominating global distribution networks and influencers

Savraj Aura

Copyright © 2020 by Savraj Aura

All rights reserved. No portion of this book may be reproduced in any form without permission from Slices Make A Loaf, except as permitted by U.S. copyright law and brief quotations for a book review.

For permissions contact:
support@slicesmakealoaf.com
www.SlicesMakeALoaf.com

Cover by Ying Zhan

First Printing, 2020
ISBN-13: 9798621928933

To my wife and daughter, Erika and Valentina, you ladies are my world!

Table of Contents

About Me — 4
Preface — 10

Chapter 1: DSSD Method — 12
Introduction to DSSD — 12
Why I use distribution networks — 16
How distribution built my businesses — 17

Chapter 2: Your Business and Market — 22
Distribution for all business types — 22
Managing expectations with different business types — 24
The Boston Matrix — 26
Capitalizing on trends — 28
Real-world example — 30

Chapter 3: Planning Your Business, Product, or Service — 34
Evaluating your business — 34
The lens to look through — 37
DSSD method applied to growth — 39
DSSD method applied to capital raising — 41
Real-world examples — 42

Chapter 4: Getting Started — 46
Your first steps with distribution — 46
Difficulty levels with distribution partners — 48
Five steps to execute your plan — 51

Running your business on autopilot	53
Real-world example	55

Chapter 5: Identifying and Creating Exploitable Value — 58
Creating or identifying value	58
Buyer perceptions of value	60
What drives people to buy	60
Real-world examples	64

Chapter 6: Design Your Deal — 68
Your product or someone else's	68
Barriers to entry	73
Porter's Five Forces and your business	81
Margins and partners	84
Your product – pros and cons	86
Someone else's product – pros and cons	87
Real-world example	89

Chapter 7: Legal Considerations and Funding Your Business — 92
Restrictions and regulations	92
Types of investor funding	105
Equity raises	106
Loans for startups	108
Convertible debt	109
Contracts to cover your bases	110
Competing interests	112
Trade secrets and antitrust	113
Contractual restrictions	117
Real-world example	120

Chapter 8: Marketing 124
Marketing 124
Creating the snowball effect 132
Media buyers 137
Practical execution – AIDA 140
Real-world example 142

Chapter 9: Finding Your Partners 144
Where to find your partners 144
Step 1 – How to make direct contact 147
Step 2 – How to use events 148
Step 3 – How to use social media 148
Step 4 – How to use Boolean search 150
Step 5 – How to build authority 153
Step 6 – How to create master agents 154
Real-world examples 155

Chapter 10: Retaining Your Partners Long Term 160
Pareto's 80/20 rule 160
How to keep your partners working with you 161
3 Golden Rules 164
Analyzing your partners 166
Branding for retention 169
Partners still being poached? 171

In closing 173
Acknowledgements 178

About Me

My dream growing up was to be rich! You see… just after my parents divorced, my dad and I bounced around from friends' homes to shelters and empty houses with no heat or electricity. Back then, I didn't know we were poor and thought eating Spam and beans for dinner was tasty. That was just life.

My dad worked hard at the mechanic's shop he owned and operated but never cracked the code for scaling his business and making more money. But for me? I constantly dreamed up ideas to become rich and did everything I could to make money.

My first foray into business was a paper route at 4:30 a.m. before school. The newsagents paid a weekly wage for each route I could manage. I convinced them to give me three. Now, this was too much for me to handle, so I enlisted two neighborhood kids to take care of all the routes for me. I paid them, but a little less than I was paid so that I could make a slight profit.

I used those routes as a client list and decided that I could make more money by upselling customers on additional products. I offered them, at a slightly increased price, other magazines and DVD rentals that the newsagents offered. I gave customers an itemized list with prices and told them to check off what they wanted and put the money in an envelope.

Unfortunately, that little business didn't last long because the kids I hired weren't committed and threw away the newspapers, pretending they had delivered them. I was in trouble because when the customers complained, the newsagents also found out I was marking up the additional products. They had a problem with that, even though I paid them retail for everything I sold. They pretty much fired me after that, but it was good while it lasted.

But the idea of outsourcing work stuck with me.

In University, I decided to sell things in person and on online marketplaces like eBay. At the time, MP3 players were in demand. I bought them in bulk from wholesalers 300 at a time at $18 to $20 each and sold them for $35. Soon, word spread and people wanted to buy them from me. So, I advertised in dorm elevators, on bulletin boards, and on the university Facebook and Myspace pages. After a while, I had others selling them for me. Again, I took a slight profit, while others did the work for me.

I realized that my method of using others to do the legwork was promising.

At University, I studied Business Management and Enterprise and had big plans to work for a big business consultancy like Accenture, Deloitte, or CapGemini. But when I graduated, the recession was in full swing. Broke as hell, I moved back to my dad's house. I'll be honest… it was soul-destroying.

Ultimately, I found my way into recruiting and headhunting. And after a few years in the business, I realized that to make the amount of money I dreamed of, I needed simple and easy hiring contracts with volume. That's when it hit me.

Sales staff! I'd never looked at that area of recruitment. Successful businesses that require sales staff typically need a lot of them because the number of people selling determines the success of the company. If I could offer lower-than-average fees, I could take on the volume. This was the turning point in my career.

I worked with clients in the investment sales space, which specialized in gold and diamonds, rare earth metals, listed bonds, real estate, and much more. Now, these investment firms are a different beast altogether. They still wanted to pay low fees but had serious staff turnover. They typically had telesales floors with 100+ brokers on the phones. They paid fast because they were cashed-up and wanted me to interview applicants on-site so that the candidates would have an opportunity to see the culture. These guys were animals, jumping on desks after closing deals. New candidates had to see what they were in for.

Fortunately for me, London is packed with investment houses. At my height, I supplied staff at £800-1,000 per hire to about 12 companies at the same time. Since these firms took on almost 5-10 new hires every month, I made about £75-100K per month. Then, they wanted to renegotiate the rates such that I would charge significantly lower fees or hire me directly to be an in-house recruiter on salary. That wasn't going to work for me… I had to figure out something because competition was picking up. I couldn't lose all my contracts.

I did something radical that no other competitor would think of doing. I offered to supply the staff for free! I became completely performance-driven, which required a commission split on any deals my placements did. My company, Core Agents, employed all the staff, and we placed them into the firms. They paid us the earnings for each staff member, and I distributed those commissions and base salaries to the staff. This way, I couldn't get squeezed out of my cut on deals. For them, it meant I had a huge incentive to ensure these firms received the absolute best hires. It was a win-win situation. It worked so well, in fact, that I ascended from a recruitment consultancy to something I still don't know how to define today.

I also created USPI, which stands for U.S. Parking Investments. It is my private equity business that focuses on the parking business niche. I love parking since it has all the hallmarks of a great real estate investment but is usually overlooked by most. Think about it… it's real estate, so the value goes up over time. It has cash flowing in daily, which means it pays the owner an income. It is notoriously low-maintenance and has low carry costs. The major costs are usually only associated with building the lot. And, I can change the prices on parking anytime I want. You cannot do that with traditional single-family, multifamily, or other commercial leases.

Slices Make A Loaf is currently a training platform that presents a tried-and-tested distribution sales model and strategies for raising capital. We list products from reputable and verified companies that anyone can sell or promote through whatever platform you want. Think of it as a job board for product distribution. So if you are a distributor or influencer, you can choose products you want to sell or promote. You can even get master agency agreements and find people to distribute for you. No more direct messages, hoping you'll be noticed by a brand. Product providers can easily attract lots of distributors or influencers to promote their products.

Why did I tell you all about myself? Because I want you to know that I've been in your shoes. I've had ups and downs. And, more ups and downs. But I've finally found a solution that consistently works.

I imagine many people are asking themselves, "If it works so well, then why is he telling me about it?" First off, I'm not looking to make millions of dollars off this book, but I find that teaching others provides me more clarity.

I want to help other entrepreneurs like myself receive the reward ($$$) they deserve and make their businesses succeed. Some of you are just starting out, while others already have payroll and sales but want to expand. Each of you has a vision… that's not the problem. You just need a roadmap to make it a reality. This book shows a way to achieve massive sales and market exposure.

I will share more personal business examples throughout the book because to really understand a concept, it's better to see it in action. My advice… be agile, think about what can go wrong, and make sure you have robust contracts in place.

Preface

DSSD, which stands for **Deal, Structure, Scalability, and Distribution**, is a sales system that delivers results by using distribution channel partners. I won't teach you how to master social media or other digital advertising. Instead, I will show you a way to grow fast, make money, and measure success by paying for conversions, not clicks.

Drawing from my extensive business experience, I want to educate and provide a deployable plan for maximizing sales, raising capital, and operating across a global network. DSSD isn't a paint-by-numbers solution and requires effort on your part. Throughout the book, I refer to my personal businesses, past and present, sharing successful strategies as well as the pitfalls I experienced!

I suggest reading this book in sequential order because I build on the information as I go. This book also has an accompanying training platform (www.slicesmakealoaf.com) to help you take everything I explain here to the next level.

The advice I present is purposefully general in order to encompass as many business sectors as possible. However, I include numerous specific examples in varying industries to make the DSSD method clear. The questions throughout are designed to make you think hard about how to apply the concepts and processes to your specific product or service. I encourage you to think through your proposed business thoroughly before jumping in.

You know yourself best, and each of us is the expert of our own problems. We know what we're good at, what we're bad at, what we hate, and what we love. But sometimes, we need someone to help point these things out to allow us to see clearly and how to make the necessary changes and adjustments.

I already know you are an entrepreneur and have the ideas. So, my job is to simply guide and enable you, putting you on a path to turn those ideas into money.

CHAPTER 1: DSSD Method

Introduction to DSSD

I like writing how-to manuals and business plans because it puts my thoughts down in a structured form, which in turn helps my businesses improve and expand. Believe me when I tell you that throughout the process of writing this book, I revisited many areas of my companies that needed work and, as a result, successfully overcame several obstacles.

This is not a motivational course under the guise of business planning, strategy, and execution. Seriously, if your head is not in the right place and you lack motivation or drive, then you need to sort that out first. For this to work, I need you alert, thinking, *and* obsessing about your business idea and be ready to apply everything I'm about to explain. While I provide plenty of examples, you know your business best. So, please take my advice and suggestions and implement them as you see fit.

Let me start with this... I have a baby girl, and she plays with toys. And, these toys are designed to help children develop.

They teach them basic cause and effect, general understanding of shapes and objects, and overall cognitive skills. Sensory development, sound-location coordination, motor skills, memory recall, color coordination, tactile feedback and memory, general dexterity, and the list goes on and on.

I recognize that these toys are essential, but I want my daughter to spend time with other children to learn social skills like sharing, exchanging, trading, transacting, interacting.

So, why am I explaining this?

Well, the same goes for those in business. Toys are much like the advertising platforms we use today as business people. They are all a bit cool, fun, and serve a purpose.

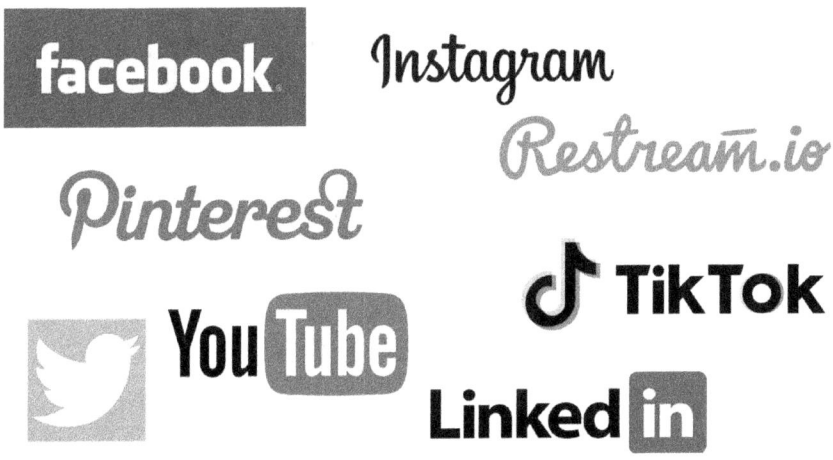

If you look at some of the most successful companies out there today, they don't owe their successes to nifty marketing campaigns, although those might have helped. They have usually partnered with another business to help them break into a market.

On one end of the spectrum, you see all the social media influencers and podcasters. They leverage each other's notoriety to access new audiences, meaning it's not always through their own followers sharing or by savvy promotions. On the other end, look at how investments work. Broker-dealers partner with other syndicate firms who recruit financial advisors to achieve massive action. They get a sales team for free and leave the marketing to those consultancies to build brand awareness.

But let me step back for a minute because it's easy to talk about high-flying businesses all day. Let me ground what I am saying with some examples.

Currently, I have three businesses. I've been running Core Agents, which is a listing platform focused on traditional real estate businesses, since 2010. Over the past two years, I set up a Commercial Real Estate business, USPI, that operates much like a private equity firm because we essentially purchase prime commercial real estate and secure them, which includes things like raising capital and asset management. My most recent company is Slices Make A Loaf, which is a training and product distribution platform. These three businesses are very different, but they all follow the same formula for acquiring buyers.

The DSSD method

This DSSD training program, which stands for **Deal, Structure, Scalability, and Distribution**, is a business plan, from start to finish with a play-by-play executable plan to make big money from your business concept. Unlike what you are taught in college, DSSD provides a roadmap to successfully take a product or service to market.

These 10 structured chapters are designed to help you use sales processes and distribution models to scale your business. And, I provide real-world practical and personal examples to cement the learning.

I explain how I evaluated and re-evaluated my personal businesses and the lens I look through to find ways to execute for mass scalability and mass global sales. I want to show you some real-life evidence and case studies of how I put these lessons into practice.

This is a great way for you to understand how to implement these ideas and practices because I explain where they worked and what I did wrong in my own companies. As with any business, I've had to adjust as I go, but a few guiding principles will keep you on the right path.

Why I use distribution networks

First, let's talk about what distribution networks are and why we need them. Distribution channels are vital for a well-thought-out marketing strategy.
They can be defined as distributors, influencers, introducers, and external salesforces, and they assist in promoting your brand and

opening untapped markets, which expands the overall reach of your product or service while increasing your gross revenue. In other words, they help you grow!

Pooling resources to achieve massive action
You are tapping into your distribution network's industry contacts, expertise, and reputations. By using them to sell your product or service, you benefit from their activity in all traditional marketing techniques, from word of mouth to using social media. They promote their conviction and allegiance to your brand, which is highlighted to their audiences.

Increased sales efficiency
By using distribution networks, you narrow the gap between your product or service with the consumer in a more cost-effective and faster way. They reduce the upfront marketing and human capital spend for acquiring your buyers.

Have a pulse on your market
Since distribution partners take care of the initial pre-sale and post-sale customer service for your buyers, they can provide you with objective and valuable feedback. Equally, you benefit from knowing which marketing strategies work and which are underperforming since your distribution partners use their own marketing methods.

How distribution built my businesses

Look at this illustration of a distribution network.

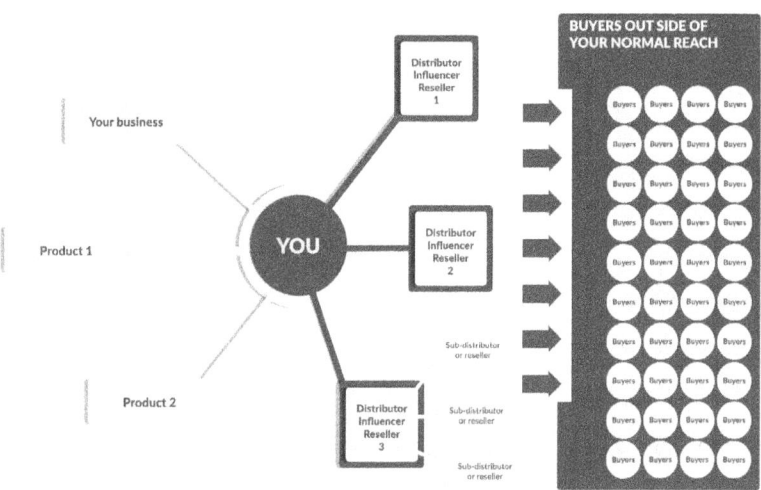

Figure 1.1 – Distribution Network Model

The people who your channel partners, distributors, influencers, and resellers reach out to – whether direct to customers or for the acquisition of more sub-influencers or sub-distributors – start to develop a stronger bond and trust for your brand. That ongoing support by all your distributors will appear to be much more genuine and enticing to the end-user.

In addition, they all fund their own marketing campaigns using their own style, so **it gives you a much wider reach with your target audience.** This provides a monumental advantage because you can also assess which marketing methods and strategies work best, without bearing the weight of the associated trial-and-error costs.

YouTube

Here's an example of a basic distribution network that anyone who watches podcasts on YouTube can immediately grasp. Look at the myriad of available podcasts. They're a fantastic example of modern-day distribution influencer networks. Simply put, YouTubers make money from YouTube itself and from other sponsorships and their promoted products or services. Those products could be theirs or someone else's.

So when a rather obscure YouTuber interviews someone notable, they are now benefiting from the interviewee's reach and audience. With ads placed within this newfound market of viewers, who wouldn't otherwise be interested, the YouTuber now has:

- Increased viewership and subscribers who are essentially new prospects and
- Increased revenue from advertisement money and potentially more sales from whatever the YouTuber was selling.

I have used distribution models in all my businesses, from a small wholesale operation while at University and headhunting services to a global, multi-million dollar real estate investment company.

The advantages of using distribution models are significant. Using others to promote and sell your product or service allows you to reach unexplored potential customers, while also benefiting from them conveying their confidence in your business. This connection provides access to clients you didn't initially have, but most importantly, this process speeds up sales. So, while you may be making less money per deal, you benefit from an accelerated growth model.

Basic principles about distribution channel marketing

Your goal is to push your business' products or services through the distribution channel partner's network, which will require hard work to establish. Your buyers could be companies or direct consumers. For example:

> **Suppliers of raw materials:** Use brokers and introducers to target manufacturers around the world who use your materials to create products or goods through their production processes. Those suppliers will have several different distribution channels and a mixture of channel partners, including their own sales staff to build and maintain accounts with manufacturers, wholesalers, and retailers on a global level.
>
> **Look at how Wall Street works:** Broker-dealers allow investment products into marketplaces to be open to their registered syndicate broker-dealers. They then distribute to financial advisors who then sell those investments to investors. Each of these entities is self-sufficient, which means they are not directly employed by any other entity.

They simply pick from an available supply of products and distribute them to the consuming entity.

Real Estate Brokerages follow the same path. It's crazy, but it's all the same, and it's everywhere. There are numerous examples in big business, but the DSSD training program is tailored to small businesses and startups.

Ask yourself:

- What part of your business – whether it is something you already have or something you can create – can be applied to a distribution model?

CHAPTER 2: Your Business and Market

Distribution for all business types

Most, if not all, businesses can be segmented into these four categories:

1. **Service-based businesses**
   Training, coaching, legal, accounting, recruitment, freelancing – using your skills and expertise to make money.

2. **Merchandising businesses**
   Online and offline stores or promotions – selling products at a markup without changing them in any way.

3. **Manufacturing businesses**
   Consumer goods, printing and publishing, clothing, crafts – making products that will be sold.

4. **Hybrid businesses**
   Restaurants – making food (manufacturing), selling wine (merchandising), and providing the restaurant experience (service).

For service-based businesses, distribution could be in the form of promoting your services through people relevant to your field who have their own buyer groups. It could be through referrals, which most people are familiar with. Or, it could be creating a broader network of people who are actively promoting your services or a specific high-volume capable service you may have.

For example, recruitment firms take on hiring contracts, and then they distribute them to other recruitment firms that provide relevant candidates to fill the roles. In this case, both firms share a percentage of the commission.

With merchandising and manufacturing, you could distribute in the form of promoting your products through introducers who get you into retail outlets by directly selling or promoting you. This all boils down to the margin available to you and if you can afford to pay the introducers, but there are so many options on the table.

What tends to happen, by the way, is that the business segment you initially use ends up becoming somewhat of a hybrid by using a distribution model.

The point I'm making is that **you can distribute with almost every business type**. It may not be immediately obvious, but there is nearly always some product or service that can be sold or taken on by a multitude of other people.

But be aware that each of these business sectors has pros and cons relating to available margin, ability to scale, and application to distribution networks.

When selecting a business or analyzing your own business, your ability to scale relies on key factors like time, involvement, supply, and room for error. No matter the business type, you must deliver against what you promise.

Managing expectations with different business types

Let's look at the four business types again and consider the margins, sales opportunities, and time commitment required for each.

I'll be honest. There is no correct answer because this exercise is about awareness. It is primarily based on my opinions from the experiences I've had with all the businesses I've been involved in. It's about managing your expectations on how you can expect to execute within a chosen business type.

For example, what volume can you expect to move versus how much of a margin you can expect to make when factoring in how much time you or your distributors will have to apply?

Service-based
80% Margins —> Medium Sales —> Time-Consuming

Merchandising

10% Margins —> Big Sales —> Less Time-Consuming

Manufacturing

25-30% Margins —> Medium to Big Sales —> Medium Time-Consuming

Hybrid

15-30% Margins —> Medium to Big Sales —> Time-Consuming

It's important to note that none of these are set in stone. It really boils down to what it is you want to distribute and how effective your distribution partners are. All these variables can change the dynamics of any business type.

So to look at how you can utilize a distribution network against your chosen business, I want you to internalize the following statement:

"Volume Is Key"

With every business, there must be something you can sell in high volume for these two main reasons:

1. If you can create a product or service where the bulk of the work is done upfront, you can then deploy it to buyers quickly, which allows you to benefit from volume distribution sales in a big way. A good example is software companies.

Once the products are built, the focus then shifts to sales volume and mass adoption.

2. People value businesses or services based on the number of people using them. Think about the herd mentality.

Okay, so why did I explain all that?

I want to show you that there is something you can distribute in pretty much any business type. You want to focus on where you can exploit a pre-existing profit center or even create a new profit center with the objective of selling in high volume. When done successfully, you will benefit in a way that makes direct competition almost irrelevant.

So with that explained, let's look at which areas of business you should focus on.

The Boston Matrix

The following diagram is the Boston Matrix, which is a simplified model for helping companies analyze their portfolio of businesses and brands. It's an excellent tool for marketing and business strategy and particularly useful when it comes to assessing which areas of your business you should focus your attention on.

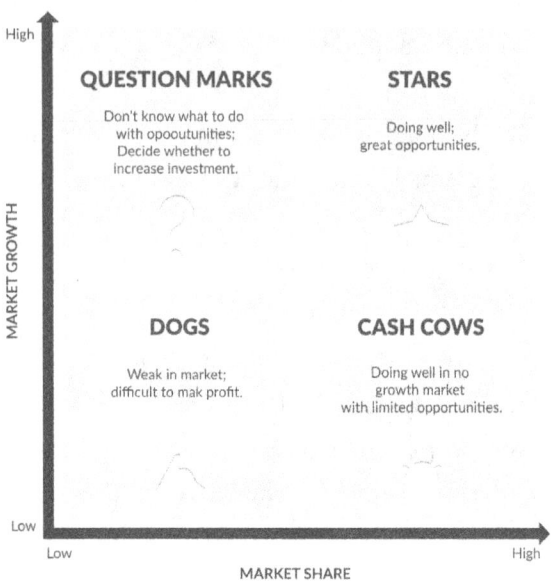

Figure 2.1 – Boston Matrix

This matrix can represent your business or a multitude of products within one business. Or, it can represent multiple brands or other businesses and products you intend to engage in.

Dogs
Weak market, low profit

The answer is simple – don't bother. Your distribution partners won't want to sell them because they know consumers won't want them. And, if you manage to find someone to sell them, the product or service won't last very long.

Question Marks

Unknown opportunities

These could be marketed through a distribution model because they can force market awareness and push some sales. However, it's probably not a good idea to risk demotivating your network of distribution partners if the product or service is questionable at best.

Cash Cows
Doing well, no growth, limited opportunities

These are great for building a stable distribution network. They might not sell in massive volumes immediately but may make up for that over time with minimal changes.

Stars
Doing well, great opportunities

This one is a no brainer – definitely go for it. Your distribution partners, much like your consumers, want something that is doing well and growing fast.

So when looking at your business, focus on whether the product or service you want to distribute has a low or high market share. Equally, look at the number of potential customers in the market and whether it's growing.

Capitalizing on trends

One other thing to consider is fads, and I look at them a lot. I personally like fads because if I have a pre-existing distribution network that is relevant to that fad, I will make a lot of money very quickly, even if for only a short time. And let's be honest, who doesn't like a financial boost here and there! However, riding a fad can also be dangerous. They can be lucrative, but a stable market is a safer long-term bet, especially when starting out. It's better to be in a growing market instead so that you can ride the wave, so to speak.

To better understand the differences between fads, trends, growing markets, and stable markets, study the following graph.

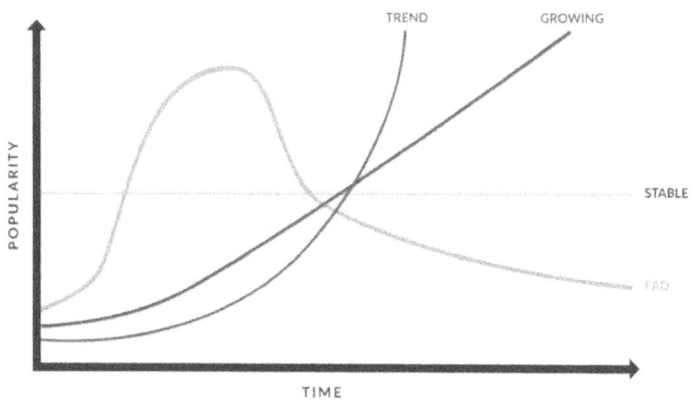

Figure 2.2 – Trend Types

As you see, fads only offer a short time to make money in. But you can make a lot of money during that time, so don't let that put you off the idea completely.

This graph illustrates a market for different products or services that can be labeled as fads, trends, growing markets, and stable markets. However, distribution channels, once engaged, can create a fad or a buying frenzy out of their combined prospecting, promotions, social media, and overall effort.

So, don't worry too much about what you think you like or what you think other people like. Leave out emotions and think with a mind for distribution and getting your distribution channel engaged as quickly and efficiently as possible.

Think about it this way… you can have the best, most futuristic business or the most elite product in its space, but what happens if you cannot make or produce it efficiently enough? What if you can't get enough sales quickly?

The value proposition needs to be current and relevant, with the right pricing and margins available so that you can sell it on a mass scale.

Real-world example

This example is tricky. One of my businesses, Core Agents, is extremely sensitive to user adoption. The company needs to attract people on both ends of the chain, i.e., I need companies that list real estate opportunities *and* distributors or customers engaged to see what's offered. Without both sides in sync, the company would fail. Not the best for a distribution model, right?

I used the Boston Matrix to assess which markets had better real estate offerings with the growth I needed to apply volume sales-based principles. I focused on distributors and on fads and trends. You see... most people already know the ins and outs of traditional real estate deals. I had to target developers in the countries that were riding a trend. Perhaps it was EB5 Visa development deals in the U.S. Sometimes, it was luxury hotel room investments in Dubai and Singapore.

Okay, are you getting the picture? What I'm trying to get across is that you can find a way to distribute part of your business. However, you need to know where to look and how to look at it. Don't worry if you don't know what to do next! I have you covered because Chapter 3 is all about the lens you need to look through in order to see what works and what doesn't. Also, use the accompanying training platform (www.slicesmakealoaf.com) to learn even more.

How to execute:

1. All businesses have something that can use the distribution model.
2. Think about how much net profit is available to you.
3. Consider how volume sales are going to benefit your business.
4. Evaluate which brands, businesses, products, or services you should invest your time in.

Ask yourself:

- Which area, brand, product, or service can you exploit within your business?

CHAPTER 3: Planning Your Business, Product, or Service

Evaluating your business

Let's recap the basic steps of the first protocols to start your business evaluation process.

- I've covered why **distribution channels are important** and frankly great for any business, including yours and mine.
- I've discussed the fact that there's something within most, if not all, business types that can be applied to a **distribution model**.
- I've talked about how volume sales are super important for your brand because **volume is key**.
- I've also addressed how to **assess product types** based on profit margins, sales volume, and effort required.

In this chapter, I present the method I use to string them all together so that you can efficiently make a decision regarding which direction you want to go.

Starting with a clear view is essential. If you're like me, you tap into your past experiences and look at the journey you've taken, whether it was business or personal. You recognize that if you had done something earlier, you would have reached a certain result faster. I'm sure you have because we all have!

So believe me when I tell you this… I have not simply whipped this training program together. It's been a tough road filled with failures and what seemed to be a never-ending stream of grinding disappointments.

It's a culmination of business theories I read when I was in a tough spot, desperately looking for solutions, and from the real-world experiences I have through building my own businesses and selling other people's products and services. It's the result of having tried, failed, tried again, and succeeding, and then falling flat on my face, and then getting right back up and trying again.

I look through a lens when evaluating and qualifying businesses I choose to get involved with. It's called DSSD, and it cuts through the bullshit.

Deal, Structure, Scalability, and Distribution

Does it check out?

Take some time when considering the pros and cons of your potential business:

- Available supply and ability to deliver against promises
- Pricing, profit margins, and cost implications

- Assessing barriers to entry for proper pricing and to give you an idea on longevity

It's important to think about all those aspects, and I can tell you from experience that you can set your distribution up so efficiently that you can sell pretty much anything in high volume, at least for a little while. Consider everything I have mentioned so far, but laser-focus on whether your distribution partners can keep up with the demand you intend to bring. They must have the protocols and infrastructure in place, with the right profit margins, and they must deliver against the promises they make.

Choosing good businesses that tick the boxes for your criteria is very important, but consider a few other areas when selling another person's business offerings. Continuity is much more difficult to achieve when you don't have full control or transparency on what you are selling.

In a practical sense, the last thing you want to happen is to take a large number of orders and be unable to fill them. Many business gurus out there say, "Just get the orders! And if you don't have enough supply, adapt when it's time to cross that bridge." Well, that *might* be good if it's only you selling directly, but if you have a distribution network in place, it will sink that ship in no time. **They will simply stop selling for you.**

If you want to take on a product from someone else's business, regardless of how well it fits our DSSD profile, ensure that you have some level of exclusivity. If you are going to sell someone else's products or services, you want an exclusive distribution arrangement. Your entire goal is to attract other people into the space and sell it for you. If you don't have an exclusive contract and agreement in place, how are you going to stop them from trying to circumvent you? In that case, you're just the middle man, right?

Equally as important as choosing the right product or service, pay particular attention to the legal elements that surround that industry. I cover Legal Considerations in Chapter 7.

Ask yourself:

- How soon do you want to start?
- Would you distribute another business' offering to cash up fast, or do you want to create your own business where you have more control?

The lens to look through

I'm going to describe how to use the DSSD lens to evaluate your business opportunities.

- **Deal**
- **Structure**
- **Scalability**
- **Distribution**

The goal is for your product or service to meet the above four criteria to promote a plug-and-play strategy for fast distribution. If you focus on what makes your product attractive to the masses and something that can generate enough excitement from your distributors, then you're on the right path.

Assessing your business this way shifts the focus from direct-competition-based strategies to deploying your product or service to distribution channels that sell to customers who are not normally within your reach.

I look for this when evaluating, quantifying, and qualifying the businesses I get involved with today. It's been a rough journey. I've been broke, I've made mistakes, and I've even mastered it within the wrong business spheres!

To be honest, I wish I didn't have so much experience in this because it's been intense. Thus, I share my experiences so that you can learn from my mistakes. It all boils down to looking at businesses through a clear lens so that you can properly evaluate your risks and what the next steps should be.

By the end of this book, you will know how to **assess, plan, and execute**. You can sell pretty much anything because you will be laser-focused on how to move products.

Carefully evaluate your deal because I have been guilty of complacency with my own protocol and have subsequently been burned for selling a lot of something in huge quantities for someone who had ulterior motives.

First and foremost, evaluate your deal and route to market *before* attempting to start. This is the basis for your business model to ensure risk minimization so that when you start, you will already be 10 steps ahead and ready to capture that market.

Ask yourself:

- How can DSSD be applied to your product or service?

DSSD method applied to growth

Use the diagram below as a guideline to see if your chosen business can be applied to the DSSD model.

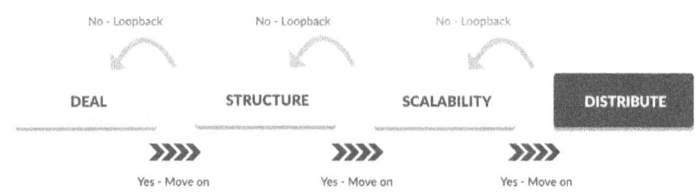

Figure 3.1 – DSSD Method

For each step, ask yourself the following questions:

1. Is the deal attractive, and does it have a market?
2. Does it have the correct structure?
3. Can it scale to greatness?
4. How and where will you distribute?

If you answer yes to all, then move on to the next step. If not, go back and try again.

Deal

What is the deal? Is it attractive, and does it offer real value? We're not talking about the novelty of your entire offering – we are looking at what specifically your buyers or distributors need or want. Is there a market, and can it deliver?

Structure

Is it already structured correctly, or can it be structured to suit your needs? Are you priced correctly to strategically target the mass market? Is it too high for your audience? Or is it too low? Do the production costs and profit margins meet your needs, and are the legal ramifications addressable?

Scalability

Can it be sold in vast quantities? This really boils down to your cost implications and the price point you are selling your product or service at. Is there enough margin to allow other people to sell it for you? Can production scale up to match demand?

Distribution

Can you overcome the adoption challenges when rolling out your product or service? You must determine what these barriers are going to be *before* you attempt to roll this out to a distribution network.

This is the final hurdle. If everything looks good, then the next step is to think about *how* you are going to shift your business and how to do it quickly. Who are you going to embed in your distribution channel? Who's going to be the primary producers for your pipeline?

DSSD method applied to capital raising

Use the DSSD method for both creating and planning your business idea as well as for structuring your plan for acquiring your distribution network. On top of that, it can be used for more than just selling your products or services.

Raising money for your business is selling in and of itself. Private equity funds, VC funds, and banking institutions follow the same process for fundraising. Yet when you google how to raise money for your startup, you always get the same checklist, which doesn't really help anyone. You know… ask friends and family, go to the bank, get a startup loan, apply for angel investing, use a crowdfunding site. That's all generic advice.

But there is a simpler way. And, it's what I've been doing for the last 10 years.

Real-world examples

This first example involves a recruitment distribution model and is something I did very frequently when I was bouncing around in different specializations within the recruitment sector. I didn't know anything about analysts or engineers, but I was able to reach those candidates who were way out of my expertise through a distribution model. The diagram below shows how I took a contract for 50 job placements and built up the attractiveness for it because I made sure I had the exclusive on the contract with a short timeframe to fill the roles.

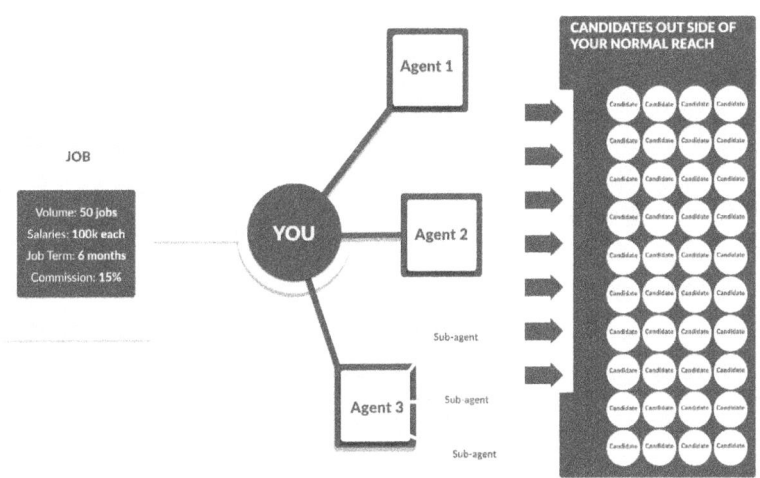

Figure 3.2 – Recruiting Distribution Network

My reward for placing all the candidates within that timeframe warranted a healthy commission payout, which was large enough to split with the other specialized agencies. I kept 3-5% for myself and offered the roles out at 10-12% to all the other agencies. Not only was it attractive to them but also for me because it meant I had 10-20 agencies, with all their individual recruitment consultants, interviewing hundreds of candidates every week. Those candidates were going through three rounds of interviews coupled with psychometric and behavioral testing. I could not have achieved that by myself.

And if you look at the numbers and averages, I retained 5% for myself, which meant my earnings worked out to be $250K. And, the best part was that the bulk of the work was carried out by people far more competent than me.

Now, this works the same with real estate. Just swap the job description for a block of apartments and the recruitment agents for real estate brokers. You can also switch it to a product with the agents being retailers or online stores.

This strategy can literally be applied to most business disciplines.

Let's look at an example with my business USPI where I buy operational and profitable parking lots and then sell each individual space through real estate investment firms to clients who want in on real estate that is income-producing for a price that doesn't break the bank. In this case, I acted as the product provider finding multiple agents and distributors who sold the spaces for me.

I cannot say this enough… this strategy can be applied to almost any business even though sometimes it's not obvious. But there's always a way!

Ask yourself:

- In your business, do you value a product or service that has extremely high margins but results in far fewer sales? Or, do you have a product or service that has much lower margins but many more sales?
- Is the product easily scalable?
- Can you scale this into significant profits?
- Will this product or service have enough margin to slice up?

CHAPTER 4: Getting Started

Your first steps with distribution

Your goal is to reach large numbers of customers all over the country and even the world. The way to do it without creating a massive inhouse salesforce, which can be extremely costly, is to use a network of distribution channel partners. So, the question is, "How do you do that effectively and efficiently?"

This may sound obvious, but I've made the mistake of onboarding budding entrepreneurs who believe in my idea or concept. They sign up, but very quickly realize that they have no way to break into that market. At first, it's great because you feel like you're building an army and are enthusiastic knowing that committed people want to work for you, but it usually ends up failing.

You must be clear with yourself that you are *not* looking for startups and **no friends or family**. You want pre-existing businesses or people who can quickly access your market.

Lots of businesses become trapped at this point. They build out their idea, structure it correctly, and plan out scalability, but then they partner with the wrong entities. Remember, if you have a good product, people will start to see the same vision you have. You must be extremely vigilant and frankly selfish at this point – **you must choose the right distribution partners**. And, you need to build a chain of distribution partners so that you create what I call a self-regulating distribution channel.

In a nutshell, it should be easier for the next person down your distribution channel to sell your product or service. They will make less money since you give them only a portion of your profit margin. So, choose a person, business, or entity that has direct access to the customers you want. If you have a good product that pays them enough, they will be eager to sell it for you since they already have clients and customers.

For distribution networks, whether you are using resellers, agents, or influencers, recognize that it's not simply a task of pawning the work off to just anyone. The job needs to become easier for everyone down your distribution channel. Otherwise, they will have trouble selling and become demotivated. Keep in mind that you don't own them, they are not your direct employees, and you must keep them motivated.

The ease of motivating them is usually relative to how easy it is for them to make money selling your product or service. Remember that while you are looking at the gross amount of sales you can make with distribution agents and calculating how much profit, they are too.

Since they make less money per sale, you must ensure that you choose a person, business, or entity that has easier access to the customers you want. If you have a good product that pays well, the people you need will be naturally drawn to it and eager to get involved since they already have the clients and customers. Why wouldn't they… it's easy money.

Ask yourself:

- Do you think successful distribution models focus on how much they are paying out, or is it how easy it is for the next channel partner to sell?

Difficulty levels with distribution partners

The graph below shows the need to reduce complexity. As you see, the difficulty level lowers along with the money available. The easier it gets, the less they make. The fact is your product or service needs to be easier for the next person down the chain to sell what you're selling. You are looking for risk-minimization, not risk-taking, and a partner to help you.

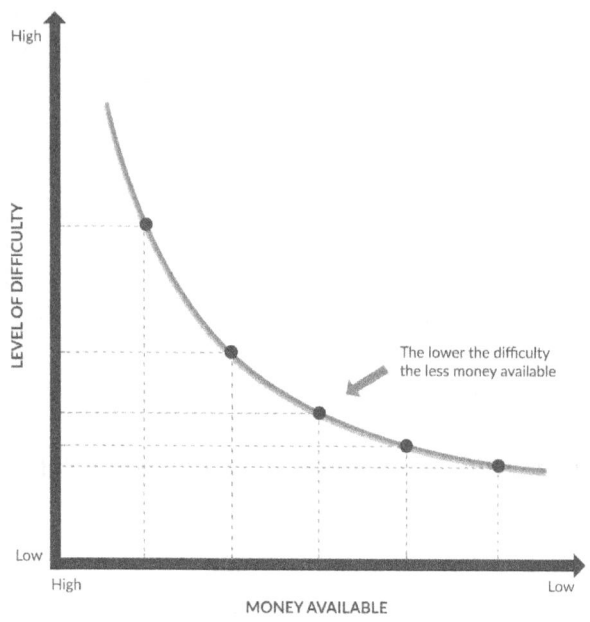

Figure 4.1 – Difficulty Level

Reducing complexity

Let's look at things to do to remove or compromise on to make it more agile and attractive for someone else to sell your product or service.

By looking at your business this way, you will likely figure out ways to actually reduce the cost implications against your product or service, which in turn allows you to make more margin. This is essential for pricing because you will need enough of a margin to slice up and carve up payouts to give to the next person or entity in your chain – **the more money they can earn results in a higher likelihood they will sell.**

If you face a highly competitive market, make sure you have a well-placed, strategically positioned product that is attractive to your distribution partners. This helps you force sales, even if your product is not as valuable as your competitors. How? Well, look at the chain and figure out what they value.

Distributors

Your influencer or distributor is interested in value as far as opportunity cost, how much they can earn, how accessible the product or service is, and whether or not there is a demand for it.

Buyers

Your end-user is interested in whether or not they get what they were promised and the cost incurred to get that.

The following diagram illustrates this clearly. It shows the buyers that have existing relationships with a company staff within your distribution channel.

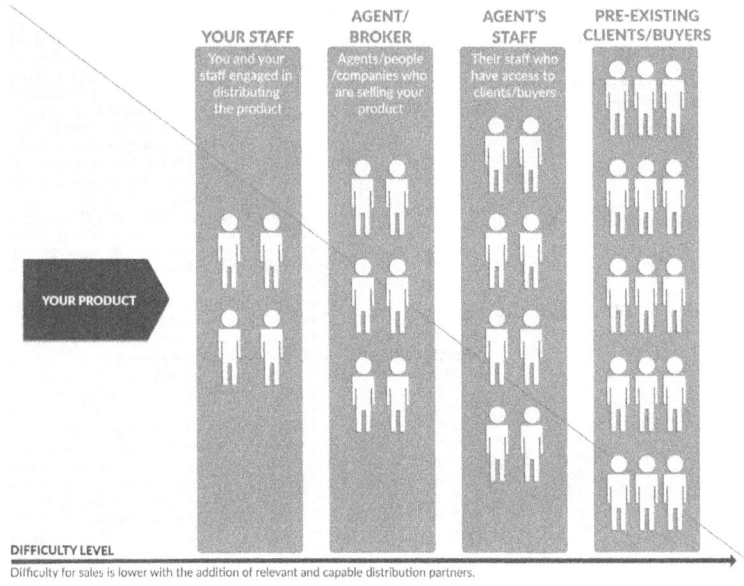

Figure 4.2 – Reduced Complexity Distribution

Five steps to execute your plan

Now, it's time to properly execute your strategy using your channel partners:

1. **Reverse engineer**
   The first thing you want to do is look at who your buyer groups are and reverse engineer. You want to deal directly with buyers you can reach through finding established, pre-existing, industry-capable channel partners. You also want to decide which markets and geographic locations you want to target.

2. **Evaluate your options**

   Since you are only looking for distributors with experience in the market sectors you are targeting, give preference to the ones that don't have other products or services that directly compete with yours. I'm not saying ignore the ones that do. I simply suggest that you give more attention to the ones who will likely spend more resources promoting your products or services.

3. **Onboarding**

   Correctly onboarding those in your distribution network is important. Start by preparing a presentation to outline the market opportunity, which clearly establishes your requirements for the business relationship. Also, disclose any territory restrictions or exclusivity agreements and set terms and expectations, especially if they share geographical areas with other channel partners.

4. **Management**

   To keep your channel partners on the same page and up-to-date on your product or service, schedule training in the form of events, courses, and webinars. Cover all the details of your offering, coupled with the best practices for presenting that information, including customer aftercare and any other responsibilities they should be aware of.

5. **Nurturing**

Your business, whether it's you or your staff, should directly help and assist your distribution channel partners. Consistently do this throughout the relationship. They will likely need help in the form of marketing planning assistance, answering questions and queries from their customer groups, and perhaps you will financially contribute to their marketing efforts.

Running your business on autopilot

Create a hierarchy of distributors. That way, they start taking responsibility to ensure sales. In the case of the pharmaceutical companies selling medicine, they have pharmacies that buy the medicine upfront in bulk and then resell to patients either privately or through insurance plans. At this point, the responsibility is on the pharmacy to sell its stock. The pharmaceutical company now has to ensure that demand is high, so they direct their marketing efforts to doctors in hope that they will prescribe more.

Let's take a page out of the book of multi-level marketing companies (MLMs). I'm *not* referring to illegal schemes like pyramid schemes, although many people confuse the two. MLMs are legitimate ways to sell without incurring large marketing fees, and frankly, they follow the same model as most traditional businesses. Many well-known MLMs have a bad reputation, even though they are legitimate, because they tap into everyday people who then have to tap into their own networks to acquire clients or create a team of people to go out and find clients.

But if you notice, this has some self-regulating measures built-in because the person who recruits numerous salespeople will likely do all the management necessary to achieve sales. It's not much different from how every company tries to gain traction, and MLMs are great examples.

However, I will say they are seen in a bad light because many MLMs recruit anyone they can entice into selling their brand. This increases the difficulty for the new recruits who, in the end, cannot sell anything. These new people have to be trained and learn how to sell the company's product.

The difference with my distribution model is that you chose people or firms that are down your distribution channel and already have access to clients or other salespeople who have clients. They will self-regulate because they are in it to win.

Here's a practical example with my company, Core Agents. I managed to get an exclusive contract to sell several multifamily apartment buildings in London. They were in great locations, and if a property investor bought one, they would make a healthy return from renting it out. I approached real estate investment firms around the world and offered them the lion's share of my available commission against my exclusive contract. They then enlisted their own freelance agents to sell these properties to their prospective buyers. Since those sales completed in quick succession, everyone down the chain was paid, and the buyers were happy with their new property purchase. How different is that from an MLM?

Real-world example

Let's continue with the pharmaceutical example. A pharmaceutical company creates a new medicine, and they want pharmacies to order it in bulk. Well, pharmacies are the distributors in this case, and they are concerned with whether or not there is a real need for this medicine in comparison to others, whether doctors back it, unit prices, logistical costs, stock availability, and probably most importantly, insurance coverage. But these companies have another distributor down the chain in the form of actual doctors. They prescribe medicine but are focused on patient benefits with earnings secondary. Or at least you'd hope so!

It's well-known that pharmaceuticals spend a lot more money on marketing than they do on R&D. While they market directly to consumers with commercials on television, online, and in newspapers, did you know that they spend more than double that when marketing and advertising their medicines to pharmacies, clinics, and doctors?

This strategy pretty much resonates across the board with all distribution models. You see… their focus is getting the network of doctors and pharmacies working for them because they have direct contact and easier access to patients.

And, what are patients looking for? First, they want to cure whatever ailment they have but are also price-sensitive. They want to know if it's covered by their insurance, ease of administration, and about associated pain or side effects.

Pharmaceuticals are a good example of a finely tuned distribution model as they tend to be pretty good at it. And, they consider even more factors to make life easier, some regulatory and others more for convenience.

They'll ensure they have as many insurance providers on board, have all necessary licenses and approvals, and production lines ready. These logistics are usually taken care of along with price-sensitivity testing for those who have to buy the medicine out-of-pocket.

Of course, the pharmaceutical distribution model is much more complicated than this, but this example provides a glimpse into where their focus is.

CHAPTER 5: Identifying and Creating Exploitable Value

Creating or identifying value

Okay, this one isn't immediately obvious because a lot of things have value. What you want to look for is **obvious value**. What is it that you can quickly present to someone so that they can see the obvious value? It shouldn't be too hard for them to see it and have a desire to act on it.

Knowing what and how to exploit obvious value is similar to knowing your market and your customers but with a slight twist. In a competition-filled business sector, think about how you are currently attracting customers. You might have the right market, you may know what your customer wants, but do you know how to grab their attention? Marketing is one thing, but there needs to be something specific about your business that you can push, meaning a unique selling point.

When I looked at my parking lot investment business in this way, I knew it had value. First, I'm selling real estate, which typically goes up in value. Second, the parking operation runs on the real estate which produces income, meaning it pays any investors a passive income while they wait for the land and business value to increase over time.

I even structured the parking lot deal so that I sold it in bite-size, affordable portions. I'm not selling entire parking lots, only one parking space at a time at a price point as low as $20-30K. That means I've opened the market up to the everyday investor. They can become involved in an asset class that was previously only available to institutional investors or seasoned professional investors with very deep pockets.

It sounds like I broke into the market, right? Actually, no. It's been a hard ride because people don't grasp the concept as easily as I had hoped. I had to reengineer the offering at least five times to make it more appealing and attractive.

The problem is that my parking lot investment business has value but not obvious value. If I had not explained the details to you, you might not have understood the obvious benefits. And that's the problem I had when initially trying to break into this market.

I will teach you how to explore ways where you can either identify obvious value or create it with the goal of having a very agile product or service that can be enticing enough to be distributed fast.

Ask yourself:

- Are your customers buying because they can see a practical use case for your product or service, or are they looking to buy because they are drawn to it emotionally?

Buyer perceptions of value

Your product matters, but so do people's perception of that product. People need to want it. So, choose something that has obvious value. If you pick something really unattractive or difficult to love, then you'll be in for an uphill battle. That was the case with my parking lot business. While it has a lot of value, most people cannot get their heads around the idea of putting money into parking lots. I would have probably done better if I were selling multifamily properties.

One of the easiest ways to find obvious value is by looking at alternative products or services to what you're offering. I'm not talking about your direct competition. Instead, I'm talking about what would or could someone choose as an alternative. Focusing on direct competition traps you into making small differences and beefing them up. The truth is… if you look at alternative products that fulfill the same or similar requirements for your customers, you'll likely find what customers are drawn to.

What drives people to buy

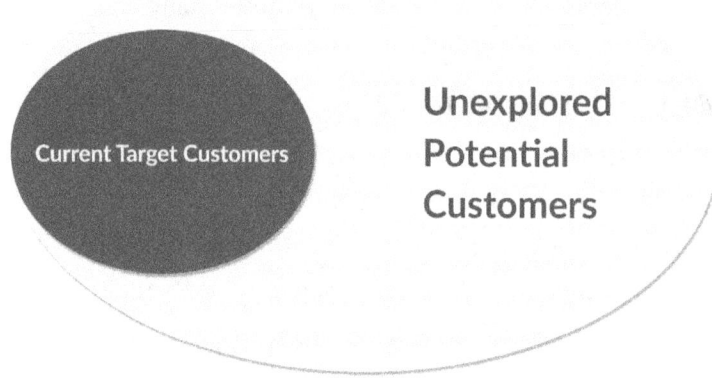

Figure 5.1 – Unexplored Potential Customers

The rule is to focus on the part of your business that represents the largest market that your organization has the capability to act on. Most companies are hyper-focused on retaining existing customers and looking for ways to get more of them, especially in the face of direct competition.

I'm not saying trying to gain market share this way is bad, but to sell fast using distribution models, **focus on how to access the customers outside your usual reach.**

Creating demand
Put your business or service under the microscope for a minute.

Is there a way you can offer a subscription package?
If you can, it's a lot easier and less expensive to sell more of something to a current customer than to find new customers. Distributors also love these business types because subscription-based businesses allow you/them to sell to the same customers over and over again automatically. This means you and your distributors receive a small slice of profit every month. Remember, slices make a loaf.

Is there an area of your business that can take advantage of a seasonal trend?
It's great to have consistent business year-round, but being able to execute massive sales on a seasonal pattern can be extremely profitable, especially if you have something to offer for every season.

I'm not just talking about the country where your business is located, either. Think globally. For example, when I sell high-ticket real estate deals, I know that most of my deals are going to be completed before November in the U.K. because people are preparing to allocate their funds before tax season and also want to switch off for the Christmas period. However, I know that in the Middle East and Asia, December is business as usual, so I ensure that I have distribution channels in all those markets.

Do buyers want what you have for emotional reasons, to relieve pain, or solve a problem?
It's a significant advantage to sell products or services that people buy for emotional reasons, pain relief, or solving a problem. The

obvious benefit is that when you sell products that satisfy one of these requirements, your marketing costs tend to be lower since buyers are actively seeking out a solution as opposed to you having to heavily market your product to find them.

Think about all the investment firms offering safe pension planning to safeguard money in turbulent markets. Think about how people seek out companies to fix issues they have.

Is your product consumable, perishable, or disposable?
If so, this puts a time limit on the life cycle of your product, which leads the customer to come back to you wanting more of the same. Think about food products, health and fitness supplements, and medication. People go back and restock.

Are there any restrictions or regulations preventing people from competing with you?
If you benefit from restrictions and regulations on competitors entering your market, you can double down on the fact that you are only one of a few in the market. This gives your distributors a sense of security and exclusivity to push your offering hard.

For more information on the emotions that make customers buy, refer to the accompanying training platform (www.slicesmakealoaf.com) to learn even more.

Real-world examples

U.S. Parking Investments

Let's use my parking lot business, USPI (www.usparkinginvestments.com), as a case study. We made the website look as nice as we could, but let's face it... parking is neither sexy nor is it immediately obvious how to use a distribution model against it. How do you use distributors to market parking spaces? Okay sure, parking aggregator sites that are similar to websites listing hotels are a possibility. But parking has a very low price point, which means there's not enough to really spread around. Equally, a parking lot has occupancy limitations. So in light of that, what I decided to do was sell each individual parking space as a real estate investment to people who want to get into real estate for passive income.

Now, I have a new market and something new to sell. Not only do buyers benefit from owning land at lower price points than typical real estate deals while earning passive income, but the land value also goes up in value over time. My company makes money from selling the spaces at a mark-up, allowing us to buy another parking lot and repeat the process. And of course, I don't have a direct sales team. Instead, I use resellers and distributors to sell these investments for me.

Apple

Think about how Apple changed the way people viewed their products. They were already in the right market and knew who their customers were. But they did something very different from everyone else. They initially competed on a functionality basis with high-end products, but the problem was, numerous other electronics manufacturers were competing in the same space.

Remember Sony, and how they sold high-end laptops and phones? Well, Apple changed the way people valued their products and encouraged them to view their products through the lens of simplicity, fashion, and lifestyle. This was very attractive to buyers because they didn't worry too much about the specifications and bought on an emotional basis. By doing this, Apple attracted the best distributors and resellers for their products all around the world. Apple kept its branding consistent, and those distributors subsequently beefed up their own marketing campaigns and collectively gave Apple some of the best brand exposure around.

Canada Goose

Another example is Canada Goose winter coats. They have a very functional product designed to keep you very warm in the winter. But let's face it, there are numerous well-renowned, high-quality winter clothing brands. Canada Goose switched its marketing to focus on design and brand identity to get customers to want their brand on an emotional level. At the time of writing this book, in Manhattan, it looked like almost 6 out of every 10 people wear a Canada Goose coat in the winter because they think it's the most fashionable option out of the available brands.

Analysis

The point is to look at your business or service offering and think about where you currently sit in the market. If your product or service acquires customers using emotional appeal, look at what you can do to make it more functional. And equally, if you are already promoting functionality, then see what you can do to attract customers on an emotional level. I'm not saying, however, that you should compromise on the quality of your product. I purely relate this to the marketing angle.

There's a saying that goes something like this, "Walk the road less traveled as it's usually paved with gold." Well, that is true for many things. But in the case of creating distribution networks that are immediately active and selling quickly, identify what direction the herd is traveling in and what your target market gravitates to. Exploit whatever it is that they are already heading toward and capitalize that way.

Let's put aside your unicorn business idea for the moment and focus on what we know people are looking for and ready to buy. Besides, wouldn't it be better to tackle that fantastic idea of yours with a few more million under your belt?

Ask yourself:

- Who are the buyers along the typical distribution lines in your business/industry?
- Who are the main buyers within your business/industry? Who does everyone usually target?

- Can you target a different buyer group with a complementary product or hybrid concept?
- What can you add to your business that really solves a problem for your customers?

CHAPTER 6: Design Your Deal

Your product or someone else's

You've already checked to see if the business you want to get involved with generally fits the DSSD criteria, whether it has obvious value, and who you think will sell it or promote it for you. Now, we must look at the basic principles behind the structure of the deal because this is really going to determine how successful and how much money you will make from this business endeavor. And once you start, you cannot really go back and change it, or if you do, it will be a difficult task.

How do I know? Because it's happened to me in almost every one of my businesses. In my parking lot investment business, I had to go back and reengineer the offering, which meant restructuring on a very complex level that included changing the legal structure. Not only was this difficult, but it was also very costly because the changes that needed to be made required bringing in lawyers *again* and getting further financial guidance from accountants. Those cost implications, coupled with the fact that we were not bringing in any new business while stuck in limbo, were extremely high. I essentially carried the company with my own finances for nearly seven months. It would have been much better to have structured it correctly in the first place.

That example relates to someone who has their own products or services, but what about those who are selling other companies' products? Well, with one of my other businesses, Core Agents, I had to evaluate the structure of every business I became involved with. I studied all the contracts and investment projects I took on, my fees on sales, and most importantly, the level of exclusivity.

Through one lens, some would say that's less costly. But on the flip side, you are burdened with the task of choosing from hundreds or thousands of different options, and it becomes even harder to decide where to spend your money doing due diligence. The one time I took a shortcut and simply took on an investment product to promote, I ended up being criminally and civilly charged. More on that later!

Remember, when you sell in very high volume and make a lot of money doing it, everyone will look at you if it goes wrong.

Back in 2010 when I started in business, and even in my other entrepreneurial ventures when I was younger, I have mostly sold someone else's products or services.

My first realization of what could go wrong was when I started out in the recruitment business. I found myself doing a lot of headhunting, which was really scouting top-level talent who were currently in positions and placing them in a role at another firm, usually the competition. The money was good, but it took too long to get paid, and there was a lot of expectation management and nurturing to do on both ends of the chain.

I soon tired of it and found out about government contracts that paid out lesser amounts in placement fees but made up for it in volume. I tendered for contracts with the National Careers Service and Prime Funding Providers like Seetec.

These names may mean nothing to you, but let me say this, they were the organizations that were given hundreds of millions of pounds of government funding and were tasked with distributing that money to private companies, which could meet government objectives like reducing unemployment numbers. I tendered and won several of those contracts.

And during the process, I learned about other contracts for employability training where I would receive funding for getting long-term unemployed job seekers into a training course and then an additional payment for getting them into work placements. Moving the unemployed to a training course means they are no longer unemployed and are now in education. The government wanted better stats, and they paid for it!

This was a hard job because it was working with people who had alcohol or drug addiction issues, ex-convicts, and unmotivated individuals who were content with living off the government's benefits system. I persevered and figured out ways to achieve 70%+ positive outcome stats and was able to draw on a lot of funding. This was my first taste of big money.

I pulled in £20-40K in billings per month. I had an entire training center, which was basically a school within an office building, and a full-on recruitment arm placing candidates for low-level government roles. But the supply ran out. In this case, my "supply" was directly linked to the government's ability to fund its contracts. That funding ran out after about nine months, and the entire business came to a screeching halt.

Unfortunately, I had placed all my eggs in one basket. The government said they were not willing to use third parties for their hiring and pulled the funding for both the employability training and work placement program. I was in a hole because I had a lease on a building that I now couldn't afford, coupled with the staffing and software costs that were upward of £20K per month. I had to shut everything down and take a financial beating, paying a few more months for the office. I tried to switch back to the private sector in those last few months, but it was a futile attempt. I just couldn't reorganize, rebrand, get new clients, and restaff quickly enough. In the end, I had to stop.

Your product or someone else's?
Deciding whether it's better to create your own product or sell another company's product is a question that has pros and cons.

I have sold services, investment products, and traditional products through distribution channels. There was even a point where I sold rubber from China to shoe manufacturers around the world via distributors. It was so complex at one point that sometimes I would distribute at zero margin to me because by conducting these international deals in different currencies, I made my commission on the forex (foreign exchange market) spread as I structured the currency conversions.

At one point, I dabbled in the fitness industry and looked at distribution arms within the supplement world. And, I made money in all these ventures. The trick, however, is choosing one that has some longevity. The point is that I looked for opportunities wherever I could to mirror this same model, anywhere in the world. I knew that almost every business can operate using the distribution model, except a few types of businesses that have legal restrictions, such as legal services.

If you are selling someone else's product or delivering against another business' service or contract, evaluate as much of the business as is reasonable. There's a two-pronged reason for this. Obviously, you want to assess it through the lens of being able to sell in huge volume. But you also want to ensure that what you are selling is not going to run out of availability or negatively impact your distribution partners or customers.

The government training program was a service-driven opportunity. But I made this mistake again, where I did not deep dive into one of the businesses I distributed for, and it turned out very bad for me, putting my company on life support for almost two years. I cannot stress this enough – **evaluate what you are going to sell** because if you follow the DSSD strategy, you can sell so fast that it's sometimes hard to see where problems can arise.

But please, don't let that story dissuade you. Many people out there hear stories like that and find themselves thinking that to be successful, they need to create a product or service. Well, that's simply not true. Selling other people's products can be fantastic, if executed correctly. All you have to do is focus on the sales and promotional element with enough exclusivity arrangements to ensure you are not getting cut out of deals or being circumvented. Selling someone else's products can be fantastic. Think retail stores, think Amazon!

Ask yourself:

- Does selling your own product or someone else's dictate your level of success or how much money you can potentially make?

Barriers to entry

Barriers to entry are really important to assess because they determine your price point, for the most part. They are essentially the factors that stop or make it very difficult for new companies to enter your market. **The more barriers to entry that exist, the less competitive the market will be.**

How easy is it for someone else to replicate what you are doing and compete with you? These barriers aren't just related to how many competitors you have within your price range or sector but also the governmental and legal restrictions for someone competing within your market space.

Think about the simple knowledge and expertise gained from operating within a market for a long time. Companies that have been around longer can navigate through turbulent market forces and face challenges that new entrants may find crippling or very costly to overcome.

For example, not just anyone can produce a new medicine or set up an investment fund. If your barriers to entry are low, meaning others can easily enter your market, then consider making your price point comparable or lower in comparison to the bigger players in the market. So, costs and expenses must be looked at and minimized so that you have enough margin to work with.

The higher the barriers, the more you can charge. The lower the barriers, the lower your price point should be. Being the first mover does not necessarily mean you have high barriers to entry. Instead, it relates to a combination of factors.

Figure 6.1 – Examples of Some Barriers to Entry

Brand loyalty

Having a strong brand image with an equally strong sense of instilled consumer loyalty can be a big barrier to entry. New companies would have to spend a lot of money on advertising and communications, which can sink cash quickly. And frankly, some companies have been around long enough and become so large and effective that they are embedded in society. No amount of advertising money could knock them down. Google and Coca-Cola are prime examples.

Economies of scale

Economies of scale relates to how costs become lower when businesses have higher output. For example, it costs Nike a lot less per unit to make a pair of new sneakers. On the flip side, a brand new athletic footwear company has significantly higher costs when making a pair. They typically have lower output, so they don't benefit from lower average costs in production or manufacturing. Simply put... Nike buys the materials they need in such large quantities that they benefit from great pricing, which new entrants cannot get.

This also allows for market control measures. For example, large companies can control market prices to keep the competition out. A large company can keep price ranges for a product group intentionally low. Even though they are not making as much money, they make some profit while maintaining dominance in the market and keeping new companies out. New companies have to price their products much higher, which may drive customers away unless there is something exceptional about the product.

Car manufacturers are great examples. Look at how some models of cars are sold so cheaply. How can they be that inexpensive? Seriously, even the cheapest cars are expensive to build. Think about how complex the engines are, the mechanics, the electronics, the safety systems, and testing.

As such, very few new car manufacturers enter the market, except for performance sports cars that are very expensive. And even those are few and far between. In the United States, Tesla is the only mass-scale American car manufacturer to have surfaced in over 100 years. The previous one was Chrysler, and it was founded in 1925.

Geographical barriers

You may think that geographical barriers only apply to businesses like gold mining or oil rigs. Those are great examples because of access difficulties, territory restrictions, and legislation. But also think about how this applies to other areas like health clubs, gyms, and restaurants in areas that are not heavily trafficked and are out of the way. Geographical barriers also work hand-in-hand with language barriers. In today's world of e-commerce and global distribution, think about how you can enter new markets. The entire point of setting up global partner networks is to circumvent any typical geographical obstacles you may face.

Being the "first mover"

Being the first mover in a business sector can certainly be a barrier to entry. If a company can take a market by storm and assert dominance, it will be difficult for an immediate follow-up company to break in. However, don't get disheartened if someone else started before you. Look at Apple iPod's world-renowned touch wheel that everyone thought was the coolest gimmick ever. Actually, Creative's Nomad II Jukebox built that interface over a year before the iPod. Look at Google. They weren't the first search engine. Remember Yahoo! Search, Ask Jeeves, or even Lycos?

Vertical integration

As a barrier to entry, vertical integration is when a company has control over the supply and distribution of a product. This is a very powerful strategy for any business to consolidate and extend its market dominance and influence. What this means is that if you have no real access to supply, there is no practical way to sell your product.

A good example is pharmaceuticals and how they control the supply and subsequent pricing of certain medications. They can set high prices, discouraging any new entrants into that specific market who want to retail that medication outside of the pre-existing relationships the pharmaceutical already has established. This leads directly to legal patents.

Patents

A patent is a legal barrier that can simply stop competitors in their tracks. It can actually allow a business to monopolize a market because other companies cannot use its patent unless they are expressly permitted. Using the pharmaceutical example, they can patent a drug for years, which means no one else can sell that drug anywhere in the world. Patent disputes happen all the time in the cell phone market, but have you noticed how similarly all the phones operate? For example, patent infringement cases are always going on. Google patent litigation between Samsung and Apple. At the time of writing this book, they are always stepping on each other's toes.

Adoption and network effects

This is the proverbial "hot knife cutting through butter" I keep referring to. You know... designing, structuring, and scaling for mass distribution and adoption. In many business sectors, successful companies are not necessarily the best from a technical or even practical sense. People buy something because their friends bought it. They buy it because everyone is raving about it.

Many businesses owe their success to getting a large volume of users, both in distribution and in their user base. Apart from my own business examples, look at some of the health and wellness supplement brands and how their products, despite not being the best, achieve a huge user base. Look at social media companies that are not exactly the best platforms, from a technical standpoint, but people join because their friends join.

The only reason I started portioning my marketing budget away from Google PPC to Facebook ads and other social media mediums was because of user adoption. If no one used that platform or service, I'd be reluctant to use it myself, wouldn't you?

So while the pre-existing user adoption and pre-established networks are definitely a barrier to entry, in this book, I show you how to build them for yourself. I want you to structure your business so that you can create this type of network effect.

Is your product or service scalable?

Every chapter in this DSSD book puts together an actionable business plan that you can execute against quickly. However, this is not a business plan, per se. It's about the business "action plan" for the distribution model against a specific product or service.

This is essentially the glue that holds your concept together. So if you think you have the right product or service, the next step in having something ready to distribute successfully is to think about the availability of supply and your ability to deliver against promises.

For example, do you manufacture your product, or is it already made for you? Is it a service that can be supplied in line with the number of sales you expect to achieve?

It can be challenging to think about the massive scalability for your business when you are still in the startup phase. And, this applies to whether you are selling another business' offering or your own. Scalability should be considered and built into the business model from the beginning.

Think about whether you need to drastically increase the number of employees you have to deal with in order to scale. Following that is user satisfaction, which relates to both the end-user and the distributor. I say that because it's relatively easy to sell *one* of anything, but to sell 1K or 1M+, your products or services need to be able to do what you say they do.

Buyers and your distributors are symbiotic. The last thing you want is unhappy customers because that would mean your distributors will become unhappy, too. That's the fastest way to tank your entire model! But if those two elements are in sync, then you have the foundation for scaling.

Porter's Five Forces and your business

Porter's Five Forces is one of the first things you learn in business school, so it's not exactly a revolutionary theory. But in our case, it really helps you scrutinize the likelihood of new competitors trying to steal your distributors and in what time frame.

Your goal is to sell your product or service fast, but you also want to do it long enough so that you can make some real money. And who knows, maybe you will become so dominant in your sector that you want to know what the threat of new competition looks like down the road. Well, that's what Porter's Five Forces helps explain.

Porter's Five Forces factors in the threat of new competition and analyzes how likely it is for new entrants, or generally anyone, to enter the market you operate within. Good to know, right?

Specifically, how soon can you expect your distributors to start having conversations with competitors you don't know about? There is less of a chance of this happening if there are at least a few barriers to entry. Having legal restrictions, industry regulations, patented or specialized knowledge, or high-investment requirements can really keep the wolves at bay.

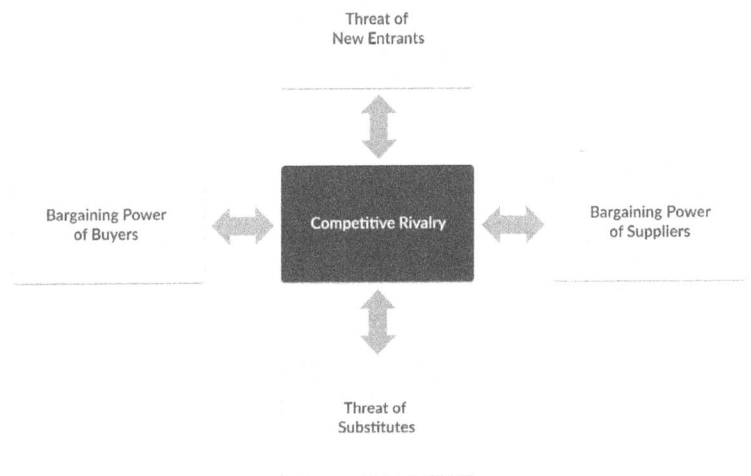

Figure 6.2 – Porter's Five Forces

Understanding Porter's Five Forces

1. **Threat of substitutes**

   This force refers to the quantity and strength of the competition currently in your market. If you have several substitute products or services within your sector, it simply means that your buyers have alternative choices. This can force you into price wars or requiring increased marketing spends.

   But determine if your competitors are using distribution networks. Bang energy drinks is a great example of a company operating within a highly competitive marketplace, but they used influencer distribution channels to reach buyers in a way their competitors were not utilizing.

2. **Bargaining power of suppliers**

   This force refers to the power sitting with your supplier, whether you are selling your own product or someone else's. The supplier has control over what they charge you, which affects your profit margins. This is especially disturbing for distribution networks because you may have structured your business and margins in a way that any negative impact from a supplier price increase could be crippling. On the flip side, if there are a lot of suppliers for what you are promoting, you can benefit because they have less power.

3. **Bargaining power of buyers**

   Customer bargaining power relates to how much power customers have over the success of your offering relative to how many other substitutes are available. So if your product or service is sold in a market where there is a lot of competition, the end buyers have stronger bargaining power.

4. **Threat of new entrants**

   This force analyzes how easy it is for competitors to enter the same marketplace you operate in. If the barriers are low, then you face a higher threat of new entrants. And equally, if the barriers are high, then the harder it is for new competition to arise. In practical terms, the higher the barriers, the more you can charge. The lower the barriers, the lower your price point should be.

5. **Competitive rivalry**
   With all things considered, this force literally looks at how easy it is for customers to switch from your business' product or service to a competitor's offering. I know this sounds like I'm repeating myself because I talked about entering the market before. But this is more about assessing how easy it is for someone to switch from using your product or service to an alternative when you are already in the market. This relates to your existing distribution network as well as your customers.

Margins and partners

Pricing, profit margins, and cost implications

Pricing is key. Proper pricing takes into consideration your cost implications in order to provide you with a good enough profit margin. This really boils down to how much it costs you to deliver against your promise and how much is left over. Structure your business so that there's enough profit margin to slice up, which gives you more power in your distribution channel. The more margin, the more power and influence you have.

Profit margin

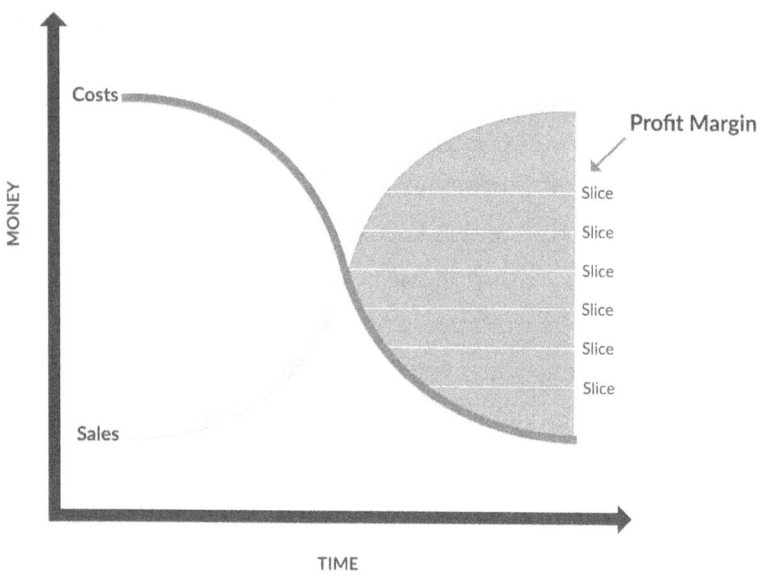

Figure 6.3 – Profit Margin

This strategy is not about making a few big deals. It's about lots and lots of small deals – slices make a loaf! They add up pretty quickly. Lower price points also mean your product offering is more accessible to the masses. Let me be clear, I am not saying to undervalue what you offer, but carefully look at the right pricing.

Evaluating the barriers to entry, in the context of this chapter, really helps you find the most opportune price point. But they also help you understand the likelihood of new competition or existing competitors trying to steal your distribution partners.

If you are selling someone else's product or service, you still want to evaluate as much of the business as is reasonable using the same principles. Naturally, you want to assess it through the lens of being able to sell in huge volumes, but you also want to ensure that what you are selling is not going to negatively impact your distribution partners.

Your product – pros and cons

The pros of creating your own product:

- You have complete control of how much money is coming into the business and how much you want to pay out to distributors.
- You have absolute control over the product or service and can adjust to market conditions.
- Since it's your business, you know exactly what you're offering and how to present it to your buyers and guide your distributors on what they should be focusing on.
- Backing your own brand or business gives your distributors more trust and instills good faith. It becomes easier for that goodwill to transfer through your distribution partners to their buyers.
- As your business grows, you can offer additional products or services, increasing your offering portfolio and opening up new markets for both buyers and distribution partners.

- You never have to worry about losing exclusivity due to a lack of growth or low sales volume because you are the product provider.

The cons of creating your own product:
- The first challenge is coming up with a viable business or product idea, which can be time-consuming and costly.
- Whatever business you start needs to have obvious value or something unique to set yourself apart from the competition.
- You're going to need startup expenses to build out your business idea, which includes all the logistical, marketing, and manufacturing elements that come into play.
- Let's face it... you might simply screw it up even if it was a good idea. We've all been there!

Someone else's product – pros and cons

The pros of selling someone else's product:
- For starters, a lot of products are already out there that you can choose from.
- The products or services you choose will be built already, including product development, testing, and manufacturing.
- They might have a really good business with a lot of brand recognition, which will be easy to distribute.

- It's ready to go so that you can start as soon as you get your contracts in place.
- You can choose to promote multiple products or services, spreading your risk and also benefiting from sales in various markets. This also implies you will have distribution partners in numerous markets, meaning they won't all be tainted in case something bad happens with one of your products.
- If the product or service doesn't do well, you can easily switch to something different.

The cons of selling someone else's product:
- You're a middleman and can be circumvented.
- If other people are selling, you face pricing wars when others drive down prices.
- It's harder, in general, to get exclusivity agreements, even if you are established.
- Margins may not be high enough on the products you like, which means you may have to opt for lesser comparables.

What's the most important component of a well-structured offer? Is it the available supply? Pricing? Cost implications? Or does it relate to how much competition there is?

The simple answer is a combination of them all. But in the case of distribution networks and getting the ball rolling, the answer is the supply, pricing, and cost implications. Competition is important in the long run but not for starting your business because you can still build a solid pipeline surrounded by heavy competition.

Ask yourself:

- Is there enough available supply for you to deliver against promises?
- Your customers and distributors are symbiotic. Will they both be satisfied with the offering?
- Is it priced correctly with consideration to your cost implications?
- Is there enough profit margin to share with your distribution channel partners?
- Look at all the barriers new competitors will face coming into your market. Is your deployment strategy aggressive enough?

Real-world example

Once again, I'm going to draw from my parking lot investment business. Parking lots are a great commercial real estate investment class because construction is their primary cost. Once built, they have low maintenance and staff costs. Think back to the last parking lot you were in. You probably didn't see much staff, and let's be honest, how expensive is it to repaint the parking spaces or fill in a few potholes? Also, parking lots have few issues when collecting their fees, unlike other types of real estate. Plus, there's very little in terms of regulations or other legal considerations. They are simple cash machines that also benefit from being real estate investments, meaning they increase in value over time.

However, the concept of parking investments was tainted by bad actors in the U.K., and they dominated the distribution networks all over Europe, the Middle East, and Asia. In fact, that cut off my access to viable distribution partners because they, and their clients, had a bad stigma about parking with no appetite for the sector. In the U.S., however, there was literally no other company taking on institutional-grade parking lot structures and making them available to the everyday investor. Even more importantly, the U.S. has a huge demand for parking, dwarfing the U.K. market and generating over $28B per year with over 96% of people over the age of 16 driving. Public transport is nowhere near as effective as it is in Europe, so parking facilities are a no-brainer.

On the one hand, we had an extremely viable market. But on the other hand, the distribution channel was tainted across the globe. What did we do? We reengineered the offering to cover the legal aspects of targeting different buyer groups. We focused on countries where other companies had not tapped into, which in our case was South America and Canada.

We dropped the entry-level price points to allow for high adoption but made it scale up enough to allow for good profit margins to split with distributors. To do this, we had to increase the available supply. So instead of looking at expensive multi-leveled parking structures in downtown urban areas, we targeted off-airport parking lots, which were generally much cheaper.

The snag was that those facilities had to be pre-existing, operating, and profitable locations. For this to work well, we had to buy successful businesses to ensure that we could deliver against our promises to investors. It was a hard pivot from the more attractive city locations to lower-priced options near airports, but it worked. We were able to attract more distribution partners because the investments were even more affordable to the buyer, while still offering all the benefits parking lot investments have to offer.

This is a pretty complex example, but I explained that for two reasons.

1. Distribution models can be applied to businesses that you would not have thought viable.
2. We restructured to navigate around a tainted market, tapping into new resources.

Accomplishing these meant finding brand new distribution channel partners, and we had to be quite creative. I discuss how to find partners in Chapter 9.

CHAPTER 7: Legal Considerations and Funding Your Business

Restrictions and regulations

DISCLAIMER*: The following information is derived from areas of U.S. law that I am familiar with. However, many of these legal principles also have close equivalents in other countries. I am not a licensed legal professional. I generalize these legal considerations as guidelines and won't be citing cases or referring to specific laws and statutes. These guidelines are intended to be used for information purposes only and do not constitute professional legal advice. Please consult independent legal advice for information specific to your country, your business, and your circumstances. Slices Make A Loaf is not liable to you in any way for your use or reliance on this guide and the information contained in the book or videos.*

Determine if there are any restrictions or regulations with promoting your product or service because they can be troublesome at best and crippling at worst.

When dealing with multiple businesses in a distribution channel covering cross-border sales or manufacturing or merchandising something, there are licenses, permits, legal qualifications, and authorizations you need in order to operate. In today's world, everything is so transparent that you cannot hope to simply muddle through the legal web. You must be prepared.

Regardless of whether you run your own business or someone else's, you should know how it's structured legally and how to secure your distribution channel from any misrepresentation issues and other legal disputes that can and will occur.

Since I don't know your business specifically, I must generalize and focus on where you need to start the process of insulating and protecting yourself.

First, I cover setting up contracts and other legal ways to enforce and protect your business and distribution channel. There is **no magic legal structure or contract** that can stop you from getting into a legal tangle. And with a growing distribution network and competition, you will no doubt have your fair share of confrontations. However, do the legwork to protect yourself as much as possible.

The ideal scenario, of course, is that all the companies you work with will operate with respect and act professionally, subsequently avoiding conflict. But when you have a multitude of businesses in your channel chasing the same pool of buyers, there will be issues. So, the following steps serve as best-practice measures for you to protect your rights, interests, and obligations, coupled with a sound basis for fair competition.

However, I repeat, this is for information purposes only, and you should seek legal advice related to any specific legal questions you may have.

Personal story

I share this story first because I want to emphasize the importance of protecting yourself and your business from the beginning.

If you are starting a new business or looking to sell another business' product or service, growing your business in today's world of social media influencers and through a network of pre-existing distribution channels is a fantastic and exciting growth opportunity.

However, this also comes with pretty nasty and sometimes very complex legal issues. This is especially true if you operate internationally because countries have different laws, and knowing which ones apply to you is critical for your survival as well as your success.

Furthermore, remember that law is fluid and subject to change. So stay informed, seek legal advice when necessary, and **protect yourself and your business**.

I touch on the legal side of business frequently because it's an area where I had a particularly unpleasant experience. Let me start by framing this section with this statement:

"The practice of law is a business... NEVER forget that!"

Many entrepreneurial business gurus tell you, "Start a business. What's the worst thing that can happen? If you fail, then you simply get a job." I can tell you from experience that it can get a lot worse than that. You can lose all your sales channels, rack up huge debt, and be made liable for things you never thought of. And, anyone can sue you, especially if you are operating in a particularly sensitive market. It can turn your life upside down.

Look at the examples of failed businesses in financial services, pharmaceutical, and food and beverage, and see how many people wound up falling foul of civil authorities, governmental oversight, and even criminal charges.

This chapter is not intended to cover legal entity structures as their definitions differ from country to country. It includes the cautionary elements to consider before attempting to start your business, relating to proper contracts and distribution channel protection. I want to focus on this aspect because I've had more than my fair share of issues, being sued by people individually and through class action suits and even being charged with breaking the law.

And if it wasn't happening to me, it was happening to people I knew. Therefore, I've had countless conversations about this and reviewed hundreds of scenarios, albeit not all of them directed at me.

Making contracts legally binding

1. **Offer** – what's on the table, what are you offering?

This part is pretty straightforward. Establish whether a valid offer has been made. What is being transacted must be very clearly explained in a set of terms and conditions.

This basically determines what either party will do or not do after signing the contract. In the case of distribution channels, you could offer to pay a certain fee when the other party sells/distributes your product or service.

Be mindful that if the offer is not clear, then the contract may not be specific enough for a court to enforce.

2. **Acceptance – are they in agreement with your offer?**
This is also pretty straightforward. The other parties need to agree to the conditions of the offer. Confirm that they legally accept the offer and agree to the terms and conditions of the transactions.

By the way, they cannot be under duress, which means it isn't valid if they are coerced into signing the deal. No mafia moves, please! But seriously, the parties must agree to the contract without outside factors influencing the acceptance of the offer.

3. **Legal intent – do both parties agree to be bound by the contract?**

   Legal intent is where you need to ensure that both parties have the intention of being bound by the contract. This is whether the person acknowledges that they intend to perform their obligation under the contract and understand that legal action may occur if they breach the terms and conditions of the agreement.

4. **Competency – do both parties know what they are doing?**

   Competency means both parties need to be of sound mind and have the legal capacity to enter into a contract. For example, it's probably a bad idea to have a minor sign a contract.

   The person signing the contract must also have the mental capacity to understand what they are signing and are not impaired at the time of signing. So basically, they can't be drunk, use other mind-altering substances, or have a mental or age-related disability that can impair their judgment.

5. **Consideration – do you agree on who gains what?**

   Consideration essentially means the exchange of value or promise of something of value. It's the 'payment' for what is performed against the contract. By the way, this can also mean that you or the other party promise not to do something after they sign the contract. It is the value to be had, which can be anything like money, knowledge, goods, or services. If there is no exchange, there is nothing to enforce, so no need for a contract, right?

6. **Legal purpose – as long as it's legal, it's binding.**
Legal purpose means the contract can only be enforced for legal transactions. Basically, you can't have an enforceable contract with your distribution partners if what you are distributing is an illegal substance. The law cannot be used to enforce unlawful activities, so make sure you are not breaking the law.

How robust are your contracts?

Ensure that you have well-written agreements and terms and conditions with clear policies and procedures where parties agree to specified restrictions or allowances relating to working with competitors or customer ownership after completing deals. This will help you with disputes and provide a legal basis for taking steps or actions to protect your business model from unfair competition.

But contracts won't stop everything!

Imagine you are looking for a distribution channel. One of the first steps in building your distribution channel is to look at your competitors and start by approaching them directly. From this, you know exactly who to target and how to get them interested with the correct pricing, coupled with a commission structure to entice them into your channel.

So being on the offense and defense, consider how enforceable lawsuits are against typical mainstay policies set out in most contracts. Since your distributors are essentially their own businesses or independent contractors, you'll notice that it's extremely difficult to lock them down with non-competition agreements.

So, you must answer three questions:

1. Can a company, you or someone else, legally restrict its distributors from recruiting other distributors for other companies?
2. Can you restrict their sub-distributors from selling or promoting your competitor's products or services?
3. Or if you are a distributor, can you sell products or services for whomever you wish, whenever you want?

Well if every party has papered, contracted, and signed agreements, they all have the right to take legal action. Additionally, while you'll find many standard approaches to securing business interests, you'll also find that the contract you create, or the contract that already exists, will never be one-size-fits-all. Each company, including yours, will have a set of terms and conditions and policies and procedures relevant to their own company, industry, and business values.

Side note: In some cases, depending on your business, you may not care about restricting your distributors because you prefer that they grow their market dominance, or at least try to. This may actually give your product or service more exposure to new markets that you have yet to tap... just saying!

Let's go back to those three questions. Regardless of what is written in the contracts, because frankly you can write anything in them, a few major principles to legal evaluation measure how enforceable any or all of the terms are.

Thankfully, they can be grouped into these three legal questions, which serve as the first steps in how to evaluate whether certain restrictions are enforceable.

1. Can your business or distributor protect its channel partner list as trade secrets?
2. Do the contracts in place violate any antitrust laws, which relates to the promotion of healthy competition for the benefit of consumers?
3. Are the contractual restrictions too broad?

How to figure out if non-solicitation conditions are reasonable

When it comes to how courts and lawyers generally figure out whether a non-solicitation condition is reasonable, they usually look into the following areas:

1. The scope of the activity
2. The duration of the terms set
3. The geographic area the conditions restrict
4. The Legitimate Business Interests Test
5. Tortious interference under common law

The scope of the activity

The scope in non-solicitation conditions relates to a pre-existing distribution network and more likely to hold in contrast to non-compete conditions, which are usually much more restrictive and don't hold up in court as well. In the context of distribution networks, the scope relates to the non-solicitation condition, which prevents or stops an ex-distributor from contacting or soliciting to your business' remaining distribution channel partners.

The duration of the terms set

A non-solicitation agreement or condition cannot be open-ended. It must include a reasonable time frame for which the conditions can be in place. If the condition is set in place to protect the legitimate business interests of your company, it will likely be upheld for around two years, as a rule of thumb. But that's a gross generalization, and while statistically true in the majority of cases, it does not always apply.

In the context of distribution channel networks, your legitimate interest is in protecting the distributors you have in place at the time the ex-distributor leaves. In this case, the condition is usually upheld but would not apply to new distributors. The ex-distributor could technically solicit all the new distributors you bring on board.

The geographic area the conditions restrict

This relates to the express geographic territorial description the condition is referring to. However, geographic limitations are extremely difficult to enforce today, especially since distribution channel networks, even small ones, work with companies throughout a country or the entire world. The law in the U.S. and most other countries has now recognized that conditions that apply restrictive conditions on geographical limitations are not that cut and dry in keeping with reality.

Scope, duration, and geographical area conditions tend to end with decisions granting a hands-off period that holds for a small period of time to make things fair.

Legitimate Interests Business Test

We've now come full circle somewhat and need to re-visit legitimate business interests, which is a very important part of defining how secure your distributor channel network is.

Legitimate interests are broad and subjective. However, you can evaluate them in the context of distribution network channels in establishing whether there is a near-permanent relationship. To do that, you, or your lawyer!, need to consider a host of factors relating to things like:

1. How long have distributors had a pre-existing relationship?
2. How much money was invested in acquiring them?
3. How much direct contact has there been?
4. How could it affect the future business of that pre-existing distributor?

This list goes on and on, but I wouldn't know without being a lawyer myself. But I am generalizing, and the bottom line is that it really relates to how big they are and how long they have been working with the distribution channel network. The longer the relationship, the more legal strength they will have. The shorter the relationship, the weaker they will be for legal recourse.

Tortious interference under common law

Tortious interference is about the legal restrictions of someone being able to use improper or wrongful methods to attract distributors or customers away from a competitor.

My companies have been victims of ex-employees and ex-distributors using malice to further their own business interests. Personally, I have retained lawyers in many cases pursuing tortious interference claims.

Generally, methods that support tortious interference claims revolve around people maliciously trying to damage your business. Improper and wrongful practices usually occur in the form of acts of fraud, threats, or coercion; defamatory statements; slander; misrepresentations about your products, services, or management; and exposing lies about your financial gain or standing.

Please be mindful that tortious interference claims will not be upheld if an ex-distributor or competitor simply talked someone out of doing business with you without doing anything considered wrongful or improper. There must be an **element of malice**, leading to wrongful or improper means.

For example, if your company has a contract with a major distributor that is now being targeted by an ex-distributor or another rival, they cannot interfere with your business contract or relationship using the improper or wrongful means described above.

For you to have legal recourse, **you need to demonstrate or prove that:**

1. A signed, valid contract and relationship was in place
2. The ex-distributor or rival knew about that contract and relationship
3. They intentionally, improperly, or wrongfully caused that contract or relationship to be broken
4. The broken contract or relationship damaged your business.

Ask yourself:

- Do you think you only need to concern yourself with your own business, or do you have to take into consideration the legal requirements of everyone in your distribution channel?

Types of investor funding

When it comes to raising capital for your business, investor-based funding is one way to do it. I am not talking about your own personal investment or money from friends or family.

When I refer to fundraising or capital raising, I am not simply referring to startup funding. I am also linking this to how you can raise capital for an investment business like my private equity company. I was not raising capital to fund the core business. I was raising it from investors who wanted to partner on specific business opportunities in the parking business. Whether you are starting a single or multifamily real estate investment business, a venture capital company, or if you simply want to fund your own startup, these are your base options.

There are three main groups of investor funding, each with a myriad of options. I cover these in more detail in the next three sections.

1. Equity raises
2. Loans for startups
3. Convertible debt

The one you choose depends on what funding your business requires. Each has advantages and disadvantages based on the size of the industry, your business, type of business, and when you need it.

In this chapter, I cover those three funding options and the situations in which each option is the most useful, coupled with things to keep in mind. These aren't pros and cons, but rather, why you should, if you should, and what you should keep in mind.

I discuss funding as it relates to the plan and strategy, but it's up to you and your lawyer to work out the details and implement them. This is merely a quick overview. In the future, I will create an entire training course focused solely on raising money. But for now, I provide you with information to get started.

Equity raises

An equity raise is selling shares of your business to the public, investors, or financial institutions. Your investors, in this case, will receive a stake in your company and benefit from its performance going forward. To set up an equity raise, you must set an estimated valuation for your business at that point in time. So, that valuation and the amount of money you receive from investors dictate how much of your business they own as a percentage of stock. This way, both you and your investors can figure out what to receive if your company sells or goes public.

Why equity is attractive:

- Performance-based
- High-profile investors
- No repayment schedule like with loans

When you should opt for equity:

- You need time to become profitable or show results
- You have no money to start, making loans out of the question
- There's no way to bootstrap, meaning funding from your personal finances
- There is a potential for massive growth – think tech startups

Keep in mind:

- Reduces your options
- Investors want big rewards for big risks
- Competition is high
- It takes time to get people to buy into your idea and process an equity raise, typically at least 3 to 6 months
- Once the equity is gone, it's gone

Loans for startups

While this approach doesn't make big headlines like when Angels or VCs invest in a company, loans are the **easiest** and **fastest** type of funding. Most businesses – perhaps 99% of them – start their companies or run them using loans. Think about a luxury car dealership that needs capital to buy the cars.

But to secure this funding, you need collateral and to show income. So, it's not exactly great for startups unless you are getting it through a bank with a small business startup incentive.

When you should opt for a loan:

- You don't need too much money
- You need money quickly
- Operations depend on it
- No equity is available

Keep in mind:

- You will need collateral
- There may be restrictions
- High interest rates
- It's difficult to get the amount you need

Convertible debt

Convertible debt is a loan and an equity deal rolled into one. Basically, you ask investors to loan you money, and at the end of the term, you either pay them back or convert into equity. This usually involves some type of incentive for investors to convert their debt into equity, such as a discount or warrant in the next round of fundraising.

If you offer investors a discount – the most common are 20% and 25% – it means they can convert their loan into equity at that discounted rate. For example, if an investor loans you $1M with a 25% discount in the first round, they can get $1.25M worth in equity in the next round.

When you should opt for convertible debt:

- Need a simpler option to grow now and value later
- When it's difficult to value your company
- It would be better to wait for future valuation
- To get money in and protect your equity later

Keep in mind:

- You need to pay, including interest
- When the note converts, you give up equity
- There are multiple triggers for when the conversion takes place

- You discount equity at the conversion

Contracts to cover your bases

You need contracts!

It's best practice to get *any* agreement regarding your distribution channel in writing. This ensures that any issues or disputes can be resolved because what you agreed on is in black and white in a signed contract. Use free online templates for basic agreements, but **be specific** so that you can protect yourself and keep the relationship professional. If you have any concerns, seek professional legal advice.

A word of warning... it's one thing to hold another entity accountable for something, but a contract is signed by both parties. You must make sure you uphold your end of the agreement. Otherwise, you will be the one who is in breach. If that happens, the other party can hold you liable for damages.

In a nutshell, there are six requirements for creating a valid contract:

1. **Offer** – what's on the table, what are you offering?
2. **Acceptance** – are they in agreement with your offer?
3. **Legal intent** – do both parties agree to be bound by the contract?
4. **Competency** – do both parties know what they are doing?
5. **Consideration** – do you agree on who gains what?
6. **Legal purpose** – as long as it's legal, it's binding.

How to make a contract legal

First, contracts are something you need to become accustomed to. They provide peace of mind that your transactions or deals follow a predefined agreement that you can rely on. But for them to be valid and useful to all parties involved, they must be legally binding. There must be an offer made by one party and accepted by another.

You will see contracts all the time. They will be between your business and other businesses, between your partners, your vendors, your distributors, your employees, and so forth. Having a lawyer on retainer can rack up hefty fees, which are not always necessary, so it's helpful to have a solid understanding of what makes a contract real and legally binding.

Contracts can be extremely complex, especially for international distribution channels where entities create contracts using different legal terminology and drawing from various laws. So in this chapter, I can only cover the basics.

Always read the contract! Don't just sign it. Make sure there are no errors, nothing is intentionally obscure, and all important aspects are included. When you are satisfied with it, make sure *both* parties sign it.

Truth be told... I made the mistake of signing a contract and sending it back and immediately started selling the product, forgetting that I didn't receive a countersigned copy. I felt like a complete idiot when my lawyer asked to see the agreement when a dispute took place. If the contract isn't signed, it's nearly impossible to enforce in court.

Competing interests

Three common examples of what can happen:

Example 1: Once you find relevant distributors who promote for you directly or through their own sub-distributors, they start to gain some level of market dominance. What can and frequently happens is that they will begin to increase their network of channel partners and also take on other products or services. Why wouldn't they... they are technically free agents, right?

Example 2: You find distributors down your channel who require your assistance with the problems they encounter. For example, one of your distribution partners is very much embedded with your business and has put a lot of time and money into their promotions, training, and marketing efforts.

Then, they find out that some of their sub-distributors are either moving to other products or services out of choice or are directly solicited by competitors. Think about it... this could be you if you are selling someone else's products or services.

In this scenario, you want the company you worked hard for to protect your network and fight off the competition and help resolve disputes.

Example 3: What if the company you are selling, promoting, and building a distribution channel with circumvents you and goes to your sub-distributors directly? Worse still, what if they start selling directly to your clients, cutting you out of the deal?

Once people get wind of these situations, usually emotions come into play. You find people or firms starting to slander, damage your reputation, or even sue if things are not resolved quickly.

Trade secrets and antitrust

Are distribution channel partner lists trade secrets?

Most businesses, including your own, want to claim that their distribution partner lists are trade secrets, which means you want to limit the use of them only to promote your own business and for no other reason.

But this is very difficult to enforce because, simply put, it's tough to prove or satisfy certain specific criteria to actually be protected by any trade secret law.

In most cases, you must prove the following:

1. Your partner list has economic value that is not generally known or available for others to use without going through improper means, and
2. You actually, reasonably, tried to keep it a secret.

1. Your partner list has economic value that is not generally known or available for others to use without going through improper means.

Obviously, a distribution list has economic value because it can be used to acquire new sub-distributors and access pre-existing and new buyers.

So, how do you determine the acceptable, proper discovery of a list? Honestly, it's pretty straightforward. You just have to make sure you didn't get the list through "improper means."

In the U.S., "improper means" is defined as:

- Theft
- Bribery
- Misrepresentation
- Breach or inducement of a breach of duty to maintain secrecy
- Espionage through electronic or other means

So if you found someone else's list or someone found your list without the use of improper means, it generally will not be protected by laws surrounding trade secrets.

2. You actually, reasonably, tried to keep it a secret.
To determine whether trade secret protection can be enforced relates to what you or they do to actually, reasonably, keep it a secret.

Since your distribution partners are effectively using the list while they are engaged in selling your business or service or someone else's, it's unlikely you can keep the list on a spreadsheet, saved on a hard drive, and locked in a safe. So, the simplest way is to ensure that for each contracted distributor and any lists you provide them or lists that they register, include a notice that this information is considered trade secret information.

It's a bit hit or miss, in my opinion, because your business or other businesses need this policy on almost everything all the time. Good news if you are hunting down someone else's distribution channel, bad news if you are trying to protect yours. It's difficult and costly to prove. I know because I've tried.

Do the contracts in place violate any antitrust laws?
Antitrust, or generally any competition control laws in most countries, is very broad. And, in my experience, it comes down to how good your lawyer is and how deep your pockets are. For example, people have been trying to impose antitrust laws on

Amazon for years, scrutinizing whether the company uses its influence to hurt the competition.

Antitrust violation mainly relates to whether or not the terms and conditions of yours or someone else's agreement restrict the promotion of healthy competition for the benefit of consumers. If they are restrictive, the contract is not going to hold.

In the case of distribution channels, it means it's against the law to stop a distributor from selling a competitor's products or services if the restrictions mean you or they are restricting options for consumers and trying to create a monopoly.

That's understandable because we want a market where everyone has an opportunity to set up a business and compete.

When protecting a distribution channel, consider:

1. Which markets are affected by the terms of the agreement?
2. Be able to prove that it's not significantly reducing the competition for that market.

In most cases, restrictions that prohibit working for the competition will not hold as this would be imposing an unreasonable restriction on healthy competition.

Now, that doesn't mean you cannot impose any restrictions. It simply means they need to be reasonable. Remember that these are generalizations, and lawyers should address real-world scenarios.

Contractual restrictions

Are the contractual restrictions too broad?
Some non-solicitation terms and conditions can be maintained, provided they are time partial in some way, such as including time restrictions.

The good news is that courts generally recognize that competition exists. As a rule of thumb, they look to balance the interests of all parties to determine if any of the restrictions are unreasonable. In the case of distribution networks, the courts weigh the right for an individual's ability to work against a company trying to protect its distribution channel and clients, for example.

Contracts will include two factors that determine whether to uphold non-solicitation terms and conditions which are:

1. In-term prohibitions
2. Post-term prohibitions

In-term conditions against solicitation
The law generally upholds conditions that limit employees or distributors from acting on behalf of a third party, especially if there's clear conflict. This has to be agreed upon in the initial

contract because that's what the courts will rely on. So, it's fairly easy for someone to terminate a distributor who falls foul while they are in-term.

But bear in mind that firing them is not always what you want to do, especially if they are producing. Even more worryingly, once a distributor is terminated, they are essentially free to contact and solicit all the other sub-distributors they brought on. So, you could lose a lot more than one channel partner, depending on how many sub-distributors they have. But address this with post-term conditions.

Post-term non-solicitation conditions
In-term conditions are usually upheld if contracts prohibit working for competing entities. Post-termination non-solicitation, in the context of distribution channel networks, typically revolve around ensuring the ex-distributor is not allowed to recruit the remaining in-term distributors, for at least a reasonable time frame. Again, these terms must be clearly stated in your contract that is signed by both parties.

Post-term restrictions, however, are quite difficult to enforce, and there's no set-in-stone rule that applies. If a situation goes to court, many things need to be evaluated and litigated against. Personally, I ask myself whether the battle is worth the purse because it can be very expensive because there's so much either side can pick at.

As I mentioned numerous times, this information is a generalization drawn from my personal experiences and what I generally know to be reliable truths. But I have only scratched the surface. Seek professional legal advice for specific information.

Remember what I said at the beginning of this chapter:

> *"The practice of law is a business... NEVER forget that!"*

Real-world example

The Bar Works fiasco

Throughout this book, I talk about the legal mess I became involved in. Well, let me provide the details.

I became extremely proficient at applying this sales strategy to any business I was involved with to make maximum volume sales quickly.

Bar Works was a coworking business, which offers office space that allows people to work independently or collaboratively in shared office space. The business model works much the same way fitness clubs work – you pay a membership and have access. You have options for your own space, storage for valuables, and perhaps even an enclosed office. But the concept works more like buying a gym membership than a typical lease structure.

Typical coworking customers are self-employed, remote workers, small businesses, startups, and freelancers. These environments promote inclusiveness, collaboration, and community. Even larger companies use these office spaces when they are expanding quickly and need suitable office space or to house temporary staff.

Some coworking locations are industry-specific and provide equipment, services, and amenities that are very expensive with standard office lease options. I saw some that focused on architect clientele and provided large open worktops to cater to them. I also saw some that focused on technology, providing everything tech under one roof for startups, small businesses, and freelancers in that field. Plus, they look really cool! The designers make these spaces look as inviting as possible and steer clear of those grays and blues synonymous with the corporate atmosphere.

Bar Works provided all those benefits with a twist. It married the concept of one of the largest companies in the coworking space, WeWork, with Starbucks, arguably one of the most coveted places to finish off a thesis or hold a meeting on the go.

Bar Works converted street-facing restaurants and bars into these office space locations. They had a trendy feel, with exposed brick and instead of going in and sitting around wobbly coffee tables, they had conference rooms, private offices, comfortable lounge areas, coffee bars and even mindfulness and yoga spaces. Everything catered to getting people to work and collaborate. It was a new business that found a niche and could ride the new trend of what people wanted for office space. Investors absolutely loved the idea, as did I.

Retrofitting a coffee shop or restaurant to a coworking place could be done very quickly. You hire a decorator, swap the tables out for sturdier worktops, add comfortable chairs, install super-fast WiFi with printing facilities, and throw in good coffee and some flair. That took no longer than two to three months so that you could be in business in no time.

All their locations were street-facing in heavy trafficked areas in Manhattan and other inner-city areas. So, they sold like hotcakes. I put together a network, presented the investment offered by Bar Works, which was the capital used to build out each location, and started selling. I was in business!

After a while, however, something went wrong. The original two owners decided to stop building locations, even though money kept flowing in. Yet, people were still paid their returns based on the revenues generated. The trouble was that if no new locations were opening, where was the money coming from to pay investor returns? Low and behold, I was promoting a bloody Ponzi scheme!

Long story short, this 11-month contract resulted in the owner fleeing the country and hiding in Morocco, the FBI and SEC knocking on everyone's door and making people sweat... and they made a few arrests... including me.

They dropped many of the charges they threw at me. I'm stuck with conspiracy, however, because I was part of the machine and didn't do anything when I saw red flags. I was complacent and top-focused on building up my distribution network and making as much money as I could. Looking back, I wish I wasn't so naive.

Yes, one owner was using a different name, but then the other owner was using his real name. The majority of the distribution network knew these two owners personally from prior business dealings. Also, initially all the sites were built, new members kept floating in, and the business looked great... until it didn't. Suddenly, everyone cared that one guy was using a different name, unlike before.

This is a cautionary note. You can get very, very, very good at this DSSD model. So good, in fact, that it can be easy to miss a brewing problem or pass a blind eye to a few red flags. You may even think you are insulated as a third-party middleman. You're not.

If you're the biggest earner, and you will be if you follow this process correctly, you will always be looked at because they follow the money.

CHAPTER 8: Marketing

Marketing

Now, it's time to focus on creating effective marketing. I'm not talking about specific marketing strategies using particular media or advertising platforms because I don't want you to get stuck. I focus on how to use marketing strategies to acquire distributors, for the most part, instead of on direct client acquisition.

I take you through the available options, ranging from social media and display advertising to search platforms. My approach isn't about basic keyword Pay Per Click (PPC) or simply throwing money at Facebook ads. I cover topics like user-type targeting, retargeting and geo-targeting, and retargeting techniques as well as how to write ad copy to generate excitement from your targeted distributors.

The good news is that the mediums I use for these marketing strategies are not all that different from the techniques you would use for direct client acquisition. The primary difference is that by focusing on distribution agents, the opportunity cost is much lower. And by that, I mean the marketing costs are minimized because the bulk of the end-user client acquisition marketing fees will be taken care of by your distributors.

What is marketing?

Marketing is an interesting topic because not many people break it down into practical terms. I've been to a fair number of paid seminars and training courses and paid hundreds of thousands of dollars to marketing agencies, even some well-known ones. The problem I find, despite how much I spend, is that they always provide top-funnel fluff with the most basic strategy. They pitch how sophisticated their strategies are, but I end up losing a lot of money with little to show for it.

Here's what usually happens. They deliver a roadmap strategy in a way that sounds difficult and complicated, and then they charge you to essentially brainstorm on how you're going to spend your marketing budget with them. It's really just a way for them to get financial commitments from you and show you deliverables to get the ball rolling. If they are good, they will show their true worth later on. In reality, they usually use the first $50-100K to learn how *not* to market for you because let's face it, any agency will be a monumental disappointment at first.

Instead, I want to show you how to start your distribution network channel practically, without blowing your entire marketing budget on ad spending.

Marketing is a very broad topic with no one-size-fits-all strategy. I subscribe to my own definition of how to approach marketing strategies. My staff in all my businesses know this word very well because it's something I always say when it comes to marketing needs.

What's the LoCoNoCo approach?
LoCoNoCo stands for **Lo**w **Co**st **No** **Co**st marketing. While you need a marketing budget, I want you to use it wisely, and whenever you spend money, I want to ensure it is used correctly.

In the case of distribution network channels, the goal is for your network partners, not you, to pay for the bulk of the messy, trial-and-error marketing. The idea is that they will use their marketing to attract their own clients who will buy your product or service. The advantage of distribution network channels is that a few standard practices and marketing principles will get the ball rolling for you at either a low cost or no cost.

Your marketing needs to be one or both of the following:

1. Focus your marketing on attracting the people who are going to sell or distribute for you.
2. There will be some direct marketing to customers to a) make direct sales, which is more money for you, and b) to show your agents you have a business that has demand, proving that it's something that works.

Another major benefit of using distributors, influencers, or introducers is that they use their own marketing styles and techniques to promote your brand. Not only are you benefiting from multiple marketing strategies paid for by other people, but you can see what works and what doesn't by critically analyzing your best and worst performers based on their deal volume. This beats A/B testing by a long shot! Also, I talk more about this in the accompanying training platform.

Practical marketing options

Let's look at the practical marketing options available to us to both build your brand and attract relevant distributors, without breaking the bank.

The more visibility you have with your brand helps in retaining distribution channel partners. And, their combined marketing, coupled with your own, helps instill a sense of trust that is shared among the masses. This is the first step in creating a herd mentality.

The herd mentality

Your distribution channel partners will use a multitude of strategies to engage their clients. They will be marketing across various platforms, direct selling, and running events and seminars.

Some will target smaller prospects while others go full throttle and look to do big deals fast. You'll find that your sub-distributors engage with other businesses, influencers, introducers, and other individuals daily – word about your business will travel fast. Your brand will be pushed out all over the place through trusted partners vouching for you and showing their faith in your business.

Once it starts, you have to keep up.

You see… people tend to adopt the herd mentality when momentum builds up, and that goes for customers as well as distributors. Your distributors are collectively promoting trust and your brand's goodwill. As distributors or influencers spend their time promoting your product and covering all the traditional marketing techniques through social media posts, their faith in the brand becomes more visible.

The people they reach out to, whether it's direct to customers or the acquisition of more sub-influencers or distributors, start to develop a stronger bond and trust for it as well. That ongoing support by a multitude of distributors will appear to be much more genuine. Plus, they all use their individual marketing styles, so it provides a much broader reach with your target audience. It also allows you to assess which marketing works best without bearing the weight of the associated trial-and-error costs.

LoCoNoCo strategies that are useful for attracting the attention and interest from potential distribution partners are through either:

1. Direct calling
2. Direct messaging
3. Direct email campaigns
4. Through video and imagery

You will use one or a few of the following to reach your target audience:

- Banner advertising across websites
- Bing search engine display advertising
- SMS targeted campaign to opt-in subscribers
- SMS retargeted campaign to opt-in subscribers
- Email targeted campaign to lists of opt-in subscribers
- Email retargeted campaign to lists of opt-in subscribers
- Facebook advertising campaign targeting desktop users
- Facebook Retargeting advertising campaign targeting desktop users
- Facebook advertising campaign targeting mobile users
- Facebook Retargeting advertising campaign targeting mobile users
- Instagram Image-rich advertising campaigns
- Instagram Retargeting with Image-rich advertising campaigns
- YouTube advertising campaign targeting desktop users
- YouTube Retargeting advertising campaign targeting desktop users
- YouTube advertising campaign targeting mobile users
- YouTube Retargeting advertising campaign targeting mobile users
- Google search advertising targeting desktop users
- Google search advertising targeting mobile users
- Google remarketing adverts targeting desktop users
- Google remarketing adverts targeting mobile users
- Google prospecting adverts targeting desktop users
- Google prospecting adverts targeting mobile users
- LinkedIn sponsored updates, targeting relevant prospects by Groups
- LinkedIn sponsored updates, targeting relevant prospects by Skills
- LinkedIn text adverts, targeting relevant prospects by Groups
- LinkedIn text adverts, targeting relevant prospects by Skills
- LinkedIn outreach services targeting relevant prospects
- Twitter advertising campaigns

Figure 8.1 – Social and Search Ad Sources

All your actions should revolve around the following:

1. Exciting distributors
2. Educating channel partners

You can literally use the search functions within these media platforms to manually search and message relevant potential distribution partners. I have used Twitter in the past, searching for specific hashtags that helped me find the companies I needed to approach. And once I found them, I hit them with a flurry of informative videos and messages designed to spike their interest. Then, I contacted them with a direct follow-up to start a dialogue and negotiations.

Once you build a significant list, use some of the basic retargeting functions within these platforms to serve your advertisements and videos to them for a while longer to see if they reconsider and engage with you.

Retargeting or remarketing is online advertising that helps keep your brand in front of customers when they leave your website. Retargeting is a way to continue to reach out to those who didn't buy your product or service immediately.

Side note: I briefly touched on some of the platforms currently available, and over time, more platforms will emerge, which will no doubt make Figure 8.1 outdated. However, the principles behind how you use them won't change.

Ask yourself:

- To create a herd mentality, who do you need to convince – your distribution network channel or your end-users?

Creating the snowball effect

Once you get the ball rolling, even just a little bit, you will find that there's a certain momentum that kicks in. It might be slow at first, but it has the potential to grow. If you followed my protocol for having a large enough margin to adequately pay your distributors, coupled with choosing relevant sector-specific businesses to help you grow, you'll be on your way to great things.

Distributors who see results quickly become more engaged and embed themselves further into your product or service. And when more distributors follow this same trajectory, that starts the snowball effect. So, ensure that you cover the supply side of things to deliver on your promises.

The following diagram shows the snowball effect in an established distribution network:

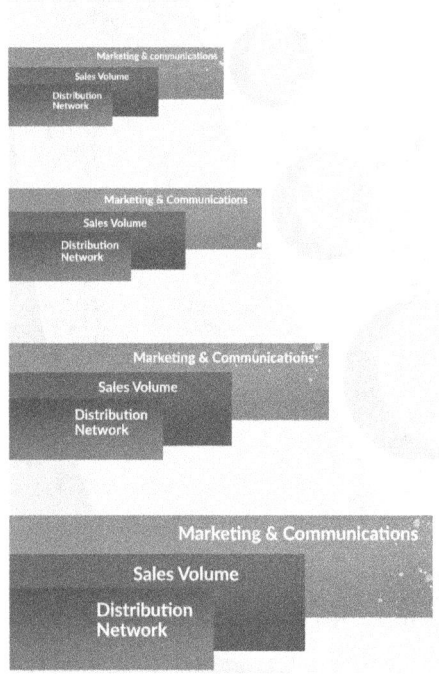

Figure 8.2 – Snowball Effect

As you increase the number of active distributors, you notice that your marketing and communications are compounding with the combined marketing efforts of them all. This does not necessarily mean that all these distributors are closing deals. It just means they are all trying. In fact, you may find that roughly 20% are actually selling at any given time, but their combined marketing efforts add to the overall reach and frequency.

Snowballing in four steps:

1. **Starting up**
   This is where you find your distributors. You call potential partners, attend or even host your own events, use social media to build your brand, position yourself as an expert in the field, and have other sub-distributors assist you in taking on channel partners. This is the hard grind, but it will start to bear fruit.

2. **Nurturing**
   Once you have some semblance of a network, you split your time between prospecting and nurturing/encouraging engagement from the businesses you onboarded. This usually involves mentoring, educating, and assisting them with their first steps. Your goal is for them to see sales quickly to boost their confidence in your offering. You may have weekly meetings with them, looking for ways to assist them in increasing their sales by things like tweaking your branding or their sales message and providing financial assistance on marketing.

3. **Growth**
   Even with only a handful of engaged channel partners, you should start seeing some sales. The more they sell and

promote your brand, the more exposure you get. This means relevant businesses will approach you or your channel partners, wanting to sell your offerings. This is when your momentum kicks into full throttle. Focus on your supply side, ensure customer satisfaction is at its best, and work on keeping the excitement going by adding other products or services that are synergetic to your initial business.

4. **Transcend**

    This is the point before the snowball faces its inevitable crash. By the time you reach this step, you will have reached high growth coupled with a good retention rate of your channel partners. You will have a multitude of distribution partners who are managing lots of channel partners, and they should all be promoting and selling with a degree of self-regulation at a consistent level provided there is adequate supply and demand.

    However, this will not last forever! So, do not think you can coast for too long. While it is good to ride the wave for a little while and earn as much money as you can, what you really need to do is think about transcending. And by that, I mean thinking about adding to your product line or service. Think of other ways to recapitalize on the strength of your business reach. Are there complementary products or offers you can make? Are there other markets you can tap into?

Ask yourself:

- What challenges will you face when your business starts to snowball?
- Will you have staffing issues, supply issues?
- How do you keep up with the momentum and, most of all, sustain it?

Media buyers

If you are going to spend money on marketing, here's a practical way to start.

This is not an in-depth course on general marketing strategies, so my goal is not to dissect and evaluate any platform individually. I want to provide the information you need to execute correctly in the real world.

Use any platform to gain awareness and interest in your products or services. However, you will need a decent-size budget because it's a lot of trial and error. It's also a lot to manage at the same time.

I'm going to skip the fluff and jump straight into what the advertising companies, online blogs with advertising tips, or what YouTube is *not* telling you. Or at least not in a clear way.

Use media buyers

If you have a marketing budget and want a good starting point for how to deploy it, search for media buyers.

Media buyers place ads for you across all the platforms I mentioned in Figure 8.1, apart from direct email lists, and can retarget them at a fraction of the price compared to traditional cost per click (CPC). Those retargeting advertisements will show up on individuals' desktops and mobile phones through apps and other mediums.

How do they do this?

The key to retargeting is a small piece of code, which is called a tracking pixel. This tracking pixel sits on a website and uses a cookie when someone clicks on the site or a specific product page. You've likely clicked on thousands of accept cookies pop-ups on websites.

These cookies allow a person to be anonymously identified throughout the internet so that when that cookie appears again, more advertisements from that website you looked at, or similar ones, can be delivered to you. Have you ever looked at a pair of shoes on one website and found that those advertisements, either from that shoemaker or another one, followed you around on all your devices? Well, now you know how that happens.

By the way, mobile device identification works similarly. Your cell phone's device ID can be tracked along with traditional retargeting. This is how geo-targeting advertisements work – the ads can target your device anonymously. For example, Mercedes-Benz could retarget everyone who physically walked into BMW and Audi car dealerships.

Yes, that might sound cool if it's new to you, but the real trick is not in the fact that you, as a business, can retarget people who have visited your website. It's the fact that you can buy data through media buyers!

Here's how it can work in a distribution network. Say my business is a fitness clothing manufacturer, and I want to target people who could resell my clothing lines. I *could* target visitors who went to specific fitness clothing wholesale websites because they are most likely looking to buy in bulk for resale purposes. This way, my ads could follow those individuals around on all their devices, and they would see my ads all the time. Equally, my resellers could use the same technology to retarget visitors who go to other retailers and target the buyers directly with their ads following them around for weeks on end.

To sum it up, you can buy and advertise to your competitors' visitors, whether it's through website page visits or even individuals who entered a physical location through geo-tagging their device id.

It's a very powerful advertising strategy, but what makes it really useful is this. Since your ads only show up *after* they searched for products, it makes it much cheaper to buy those ads. You can literally target the competition's potential customers.

Practical execution – AIDA

Since you will be writing or at least having someone else prepare your advertising messages and ads, I must discuss copywriting. First, you need a basic structure to follow for your ad copy, which you can refer to at any time. I like the AIDA model – Attention, Interest, Desire, Action. I learned it in University, and it's so easy to remember and very effective. Whenever I look to create email campaigns or even the flow of a sales video, I follow AIDA.

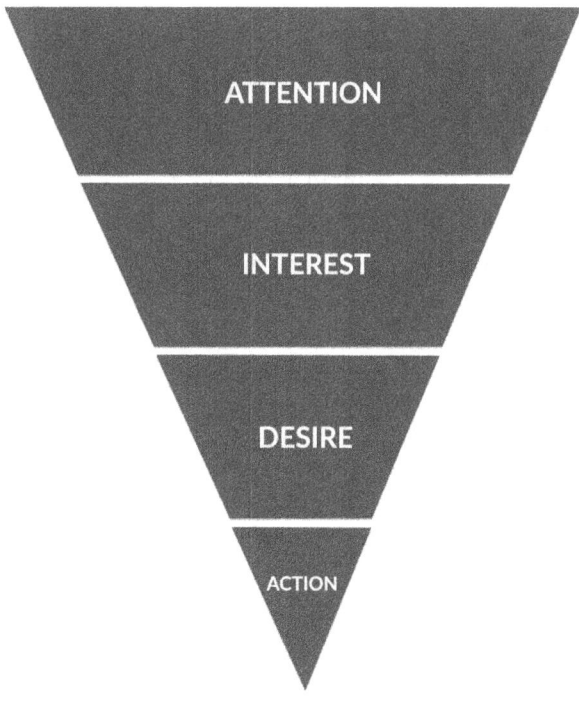

Figure 8.3 – AIDA Model

Attention

As obvious as it sounds, the first thing you need to accomplish with any piece of advertising, whether text or video, is to capture the viewer's attention. The first paragraph of text or dialogue must be the strongest part of your message. Consider using a mixture of colors, pictures, and exciting or impressive video footage to create an immediate and lasting impression.

Interest

Once you've successfully grabbed the viewer's attention, you have to spark interest to keep them hooked. Remember, you are trying to sell someone something, and they know that. So, their mental barriers are up. Think about ways or things you can say to establish a personal link or emotional desire for them to want to know more about what problem you are solving. Highlight something special. Can you allude to a secret or something that's going to happen in the future, called future pacing, and then set up a big reveal? This keeps them on the hook, wanting more.

Desire

If the viewer has made it this far, they probably like what they see. Now, you should pivot toward the sale by making a logical case. Create desire and prove to the viewer why they absolutely have to have your product or service. I find the best way to do this is by showing how you can solve the problem you presented to them and that the solution is as simple as buying what you're offering. Tell them what they are going to get.

Action

At this point, tell them how to get what you are offering. This is your call to action (CTA). Absolutely every piece of ad copy and video and audio advertisement must have a CTA. There must always be an offer! You can even try to instill a sense of urgency by offering a promotion or special offer with a limited-time or unique arrangement if they act early. Whatever this is, it needs to be relevant to your product or service and as powerful as grabbing their attention in the first place.

Real-world example

I wanted to cover the depth of advertising options available, but in reality, the focus is actually elsewhere. I just don't want you to think that I am unaware of the more sophisticated marketing channels available. This is not a competition on what works best. Cherry-picking is what is required and necessary to generate excitement within your distribution channel. If they are going to sell your product, they will engage in their own marketing funnels. The point is that you want them to cover the larger marketing budgets collectively.

For example, my parking investment business has limitations on what we can market and where. This is linked to what is allowed to be marketed concerning securities laws, restrictions, and regulations. So, the sales volume revolves around the human capital behind the hardware. There's a heavy requirement of consultancy involved, which is why structuring a business so that it's suitable for a distribution model works so well.

If you have 20+ people marketing your business, coupled with making direct sales, your exposure and brand identity will increase exponentially without you bearing the direct cost of it. Essentially, you are spreading the risk.

When using a distribution network, you don't want to spend too much time on the funnel. Rather, focus on minimizing the advertising spend.

CHAPTER 9: Finding Your Partners

Where to find your partners

If you already have a few connections and know of some businesses that could assist you in getting your distribution channel started, then the obvious move is to contact them first.

However, I'm going to assume that you don't know anyone, or you've used the connections you already have and need to restart your search for new distribution channel partners. These grassroots strategies will get you started, but their results are only as good as the effort you put into them.

The strategy for finding, pitching, and signing distributing agents is pretty simple.

First, you make contact, pitch what you're promoting, and tell them how much they can make. Try and pop up on their radar as much as possible using some or all the marketing techniques we covered in Chapter 8. Target and retarget them with display advertising so that you appear on their devices, websites, apps, and social media feeds constantly. Using this technique, when you reach out to them, they will already know who you are.

But to make this work without wasting time and money, create a list of potential targets. I know a few ways and tricks to do this, which I cover in detail in the upcoming sections.

How to look attractive to distributors

To find and attract distribution channel partners, remember what you are offering them. Despite how much you think you need them at this point, you need to think about what you offer them and **why they should work with you.**

Think of these sector-specific businesses or independent contractors as influencers, introducers, and freelance salespeople. To resonate with them, lead with a powerful statement showing them the money they can make and that it will be something they can do with relative ease.

If they can distribute for you, explain how much they will make from the channel partners they bring on board. Your goal is to attract as many distribution network partners as you can in order to create a snowball effect for your revenue streams.

Distributors are everywhere, and I mentioned a few examples earlier, including introducers, influencers, retail outlets, and online stores. But any individual or business that works with you to generate sales is part of your distribution channel. They could be both establishing additional channel partners or actually selling directly to your buyer groups. The question is, how are you going to approach them?

Before starting the hunt, cover these three things:

1. **Establish your target distributors**

   I say this numerous times throughout this book… you want to talk to people and businesses that are relevant to your sector. These entities will know and understand what you are selling and have pre-established buyer groups or other channel partners who can meet your objectives. You **must qualify your prospects**, as with any sale. Ensure that they are relevant to you so that when they start, both of you benefit immediately.

2. **Have support frameworks in place**

   A solid support framework is essential for onboarding your channel partners after that first contact. Proper marketing materials, training manuals, and FAQs are basic requirements. Think about how that interaction will go. If they are interested, they will ask for information about your business. The more support and infrastructure you can demonstrate, the higher the likelihood of them signing up.

3. **Sell yourself – people need to like you**

   People and companies want to work with people they like, and it's no different when it comes to establishing your network. You might have a great product or service, but if people are not drawn to you or dislike you, you will have a hard time recruiting channel partners.

Step 1 – How to make direct contact

To grow your network of distribution partners, get used to picking up the phone and calling them directly. It's the fastest way to make immediate contact and present your offer. If you choose a distributor relevant to your sector, they will likely hear you out. Remember, they are in the business to make money!

Your immediate goal is to get in front of a decision-maker and turn that interruption into an interaction. Think about it like this… you call to discuss a business arrangement. You are not selling them anything directly, albeit you are selling yourself and your proposal.

I spent weeks and even months calling all the businesses I could find around the world. It was hard work, but it paid off. You tend to do this in bursts because once you have a handful of potential distribution partners interested, you switch gears and focus on driving the ones you have into action.

Better still, set up sub-distribution or master agent contracts that allow those businesses to find other channel partners, too. You need proper targeting, a good script, and a lot of drive, but that's why you are here, right? This work will make you a lot of money, so put away any reservations you may have about cold calling.

Step 2 – How to use events

Events are fantastic ways to build your agent distribution network. I used to set up events myself or go to pre-established sector-specific events and book a slot to present all the time. They work so well because everyone in attendance is already primed and ready to hear what you have to offer. I did these events around the world in places where I knew my offering would be considered novel and new.

You can start small. I hosted them in hotel seminar rooms or rented space in serviced offices, using websites like meetup.com and eventbrite.com to advertise the events. The results were tremendous. Even if only 20 people attended and 1 person signed on, that was a win, especially if they started promoting and selling my product soon after. Your goal is to inform, educate, and excite.

Do these as often as you can. I used to book them every Thursday evening so that no matter what, every week I had an opportunity to speak face-to-face with people while controlling the environment.

Step 3 – How to use social media

I discussed the use of social media in Chapter 8. The bottom line is that everyone is on social media platforms today, and you don't always have to use paid promotions to attract attention. These platforms use algorithms to prioritize organic content. It changes from year to year, so I can't present something as the gold standard.

At the time of writing this book, live video is being heavily prioritized by many social media platforms in terms of how their algorithms prioritize certain types of content. In the beginning, all you had to do was post a comment. Next, imagery was prioritized over text posts, and then recorded video and finally live streams. It's ever-evolving.

Also, search functions find people by interests, location, and other filters that can help you find channel partners. I used Twitter, LinkedIn, and Facebook to find overseas real estate investment professionals. People always like to brag about their titles, so it was easy to find them. You do not even have to reach out to them on social media. You can find out what company they work for or businesses they own and contact them through the appropriate channels.

On the flip side, depending on your product, be selective about the medium you choose to make contact on. For example, if you are a fitness brand looking for influencers, perhaps a direct message is more appropriate because they can view your business immediately and check out what you're selling. Think of the titles of the individuals you want to connect with in companies or sectors.

Step 4 – How to use Boolean search

Boolean search takes me back to my recruiting days when I first discovered it. It really is the bread and butter when it comes to effective search and selection today, where almost everyone you want to interact with has a profile on the internet.

Boolean is search logic that can be used in Google, Bing, resume databases, and even some social media platforms like Facebook and LinkedIn. It gives you the ability to string a complex query and pull together all that information in one click. I do this periodically just to see who and what comes up.

Quick note: The Boolean strings below do not work in the same way on Facebook since they removed their Graph Search. Facebook now allows you to do a simple semantic search within the Facebook Search Omnibox to get results. For example, type in "Yoga Personal Training New York," and you get a list of people who meet that criteria.

A fully constructed Boolean string can look quite confusing at first, but honestly, it really isn't complicated. You'll probably understand its purpose quickly after a brief explanation. There are only six elements to remember:

1. **AND**
    Using AND combines key words
    E.g., Fitness AND Health AND Nutrition

2. **OR**

    Using OR broadens a search to include any of the keywords

    E.g., Fitness AND Health AND Nutrition AND (Manhattan OR Boston)

3. **NOT**

    Using NOT will narrow your search by excluding specific keywords

    E.g., Fitness AND Health AND Nutrition AND (Manhattan OR Boston) AND NOT (Yoga OR Pilates)

4. **( )**

    Using parentheses helps you create a more complex search

    E.g., (Manhattan OR Boston) AND (Yoga OR Pilates)

5. **" "**

    Use quotes to search for an exact phrase

    E.g., "Hot Yoga" AND (Boston OR Manhattan OR Chicago)

6. *****

    Using an asterisk in place of a character allows the search engine to substitute the * with any number of letters or characters to finish the word

    E.g., Educat* returns results like educat**e**, educat**ed**, educat**ion**, educat**ional**, or educat**or**.

These elements, coupled with the keywords you are looking for, can create a massive range of results that may surprise you. The reason I do so well in this business is that I come from the world of recruiting, where finding humans relevant to specific criteria was the job.

Let's look at an example of a search query. In this example, I want to sell fitness apparel that is designed specifically with Hot Yoga in mind. Thinking about our distribution model, it would make sense for me to look for people who could act as resellers or influencers to promote my fitness apparel to people they know. My targets could be yoga enthusiasts and yoga instructors.

My search query could be:

"Hot Yoga" AND Health AND Fitness

OR

"Hot Yoga" AND Health AND Fitness AND Instruct*

These queries are extremely effective in Facebook, LinkedIn, and resume databases like Monster.com. There are many ways to search and select potential distribution partners, but I personally love this strategy the most. You see… when people describe and promote themselves on Facebook, a job board, resume database, or professional network platform like LinkedIn, they showcase exactly what they say they are capable of.

Searching this way allows you to find people who match the keywords you choose. You can see which companies they work for, what they did in those companies, how long they worked there, and usually, you get either their direct contact details or have a way to send a direct message. Along with that, when you find the people with the skill sets and sector specialties you want, these databases usually allow you to search all the other people who list that profession in that particular company or region.

That's how I used to headhunt potential candidates in recruitment and for sector-proficient potential partners for my distribution networks.

Step 5 – How to build authority

Take, for example, some of the influencers you see on social media today. They make lots of money by either selling directly or recruiting other influencers to sell their products or services. The reason they can distribute so effectively is that they have a trusted following, and they recruit other influencers to promote to their trusted following.

This demonstrates that you do not have to be an expert in something. Instead, you could be a powerful brand ambassador of your or someone else's product or service.

I make this distinction because people sometimes become trapped, thinking that to be an authority, you have to know everything. When I switched from the recruiting distribution model to focus on international real estate, I didn't understand that much about real estate. I now know a lot because, through constant engagement with that network and as my business grew, I was forced to learn. The good news was that I made money at the same time. That's the beauty of channel partners specific to your business sector. You benefit from their expertise, which educates you and makes you money at the same time.

For example, through ongoing conversations, I learned about one of my distributor's market conditions in China. I then contacted the next channel partner on my list, which I was either prospecting or nurturing, and relayed the information I learned. While I learned something new, I immediately capitalized on it through the next interaction, where I could instill a sense of expertise. This is extremely important because your distribution partners want to know that they are working for someone who is knowledgeable, which subsequently increases their confidence and faith in your offerings.

Step 6 – How to create master agents

Finding or creating master agents is an incredibly powerful strategy that links back to what we discussed about difficulties with distribution partners. After you get the ball rolling, you will find it extremely profitable to bring on sub-distributors. They will likely be the channel partners you already know who are gaining momentum.

And, they probably know other companies in the sector that they can refer you to and will have an immediate impact.

This strategy closely resembles employee referral programs in traditional businesses and gives you many of the same benefits, which include the following:

1. You get higher quality partners
2. You decrease the time to acquire partners
3. There is a decrease in partner turnover rates
4. The cost of acquisition is reduced

This is really where we start feeling the snowball effect, where you can have hundreds of distributors all marketing and promoting for you while under the management of other sub-distributors in your network. It can become a self-regulating money-making machine. It is the rocket fuel that boosts your network incredibly fast!

Be sure you can keep up with the demand because if not, your business will start to falter, and it can kill the momentum in a heartbeat. Use the accompanying training platform (www.slicesmakealoaf.com) to drive home the lessons presented in this book.

Real-world examples

In this case study, let's use the example of you being in the Health and Fitness sector, and the product line you are promoting is an energy drink in powdered form that has roughly 30 servings per container.

Each container is $30, and your profit margin for each one works out to roughly $6, after the cost of manufacturing, shipping, and how much you pay your distributors and influencers to promote and sell. The following figures are based on the second or third month when your network is established.

- You have 500 entities, comprised of influencers, promotors, and online and offline retail outlets, promoting your product. You use the 80/20 rule, which roughly means 20% are actively promoting on any given day.
- That means that you have 100 people promoting through their own social media platforms and retail outlets to their potential client base on any given day.
- Let's say that they each have on average – and this is on the low end – 1,000 trusted followers on social media or their own previous buyers and clients.
- Let's say 20% of them (200) view the product and 20% of those (40) think about buying and 20% (8) actually buy. That means you have 100 x 8 sales each, which is 800 sales per day.
- 800 sales per day at $6 works out to $4,800 per day or $144,000 every 30 days.

That was a product-specific example of what you can expect with distribution channels. And frankly, I used low ranges. For example, most of you know that active influencers have lot more than 1,000 followers!

What's more important is something that isn't immediately obvious – you are promoting your product through trusted referral agents/distributors to over 100,000 potential buyers on any given day and achieving a 0.8% close rate, which works out to 800 closed deals. But you are also building awareness, which you are not directly paying for. Those marketing costs are paid for by the distributors. Think about how you and your distribution channel partners can retarget those 99,200 non-buyers.

You are simultaneously creating a really strong brand identity and forcing market awareness in a way that pays you at the same time.

True story
You may think that the energy drink example was unrealistic. But let me tell you, I have used this strategy selling commercial real estate around the world. I onboarded roughly 200 international real estate investment firms who sold over $100M in real estate in under 12 months, where I took an average commission of 3%. I made $3M in commissions before I ran out of stock, which was related to the demand for that particular type of commercial real estate.

You see... the snowball effect finds its home in the way distribution channels work. They promote trust. As distributors and influencers promote your product and cover all the traditional marketing techniques through social media posts, their faith in the brand becomes more visible. The people they reach out to develop a stronger bond and trust as well.

This creates a constant stream of new distributors wanting to jump on the same bandwagon. Your target end-users now see your brand represented by many trusted parties. It's one thing to get your network up and running but an entirely different thing to ensure you are delivering against what you promised.

CHAPTER 10: Retaining Your Partners Long Term

Pareto's 80/20 rule

I find Pareto's rule to be valid every time I engage with other businesses to help promote my products or services. The entire network tends to cycle with the 80/20 rule. Roughly 20% of those in the distribution channel are executing sales at any given time, with the other 80% either standing idle or waiting for their marketing or promotional efforts to kick in.

The best part is that while the flow may only come from 20% of your network, all 100% of them will be marketing your brand, which means your customer reach and the number of times they are retargeted will be through the roof. More and more dialogues will take place, more word-of-mouth marketing, more referrals, more sharing, more everything!

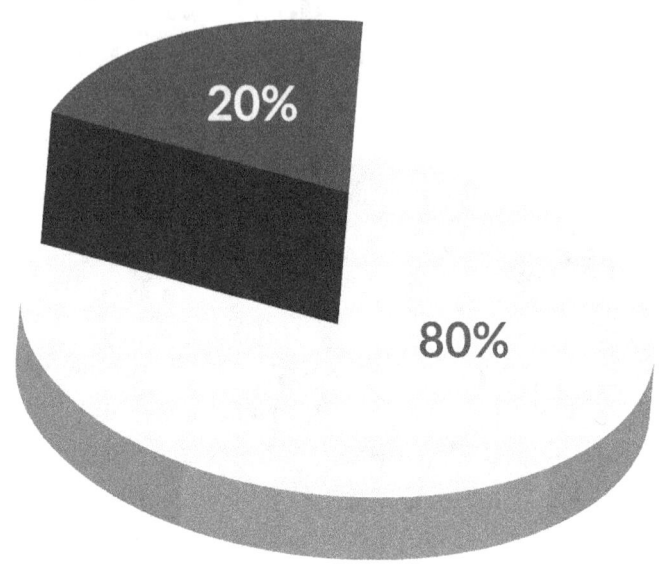

Figure 10.1 – 80/20 Rule

How to keep your partners working with you

First of all, you must **keep your partners excited.** The idea is to nurture, nurture, nurture. You want your distribution channel partners to have the easiest time possible when selling or promoting your brand. They should feel that it's easy, rewarding, and safe, knowing that their customers and connections are getting exactly what they want.

Think about how you can help them achieve that. For example, if they are struggling, let them know what's working well for your other distributors. Be consistent with interactions revolving around training and education, coupled with future pacing and keeping them informed about what's on the horizon. Achieve this through things like events, creating new products or services, new variations, complementary products or services, and special offers.

Having many distributors creates a lot of brand awareness, so you will likely receive numerous direct inquiries. This presents an excellent opportunity, and I swear by the following approach. Rather than keep the direct deals yourself, pass them on to your network. Keep your partners loving you. It's okay to provide some easy wins to your best or perhaps even struggling distributors. Make them feel valued because sometimes throwing a few easy wins their way further strengthens their relationship with you.

Understanding the fickle nature of your network
Unfortunately, distribution channel partners are notoriously fickle. We covered how fickle they can be from a legal standpoint in Chapter 7. They will always be open to taking on another competing product, much like the way they started working for you. All they need is a solid pitch and good margins to work with.

This becomes especially true as they start establishing dominance in their own markets and become more empowered. They are probably earning a lot of money and marketing to build their own businesses and are now thinking about how they can make even more by selling other complementary products.

So, it's critical that you structurally and contractually enforce as much as is reasonable regarding the agreement you have with your distribution partners.

But look at it from the other side. Depending on your business, you may not care about restricting your distributors from taking on other products. As long as they are not abandoning your product or service, why not let them grow their market dominance and, in doing so, giving your product or service more exposure to new markets you have not tapped into yet.

How to cultivate solid relationships with your channel partners

Nurturing and strengthening solid relationships with your distribution channel partners is essential to benefit from all the work you put into this business. You can't afford to lose your network by being complacent. Look to develop and maintain strong relationships among your employees and your buyers. But in distribution network channels, it's equally important to maintain those relationships with your distributors, too. It's easy to forget that they need attention since you are essentially sharing your profits with them... you'd think paying them is enough. Trust me, it isn't!

The relationship you have with your distribution channel partners is absolutely essential to the success of your business. Think about it... without them, you wouldn't be selling at that level or in those markets. They are marketing your business, even if they are not doing a great job of closing deals. You still benefit from brand awareness that you would not otherwise have.

When you experience success

As soon as you gain a little momentum, there comes a point when you take on competition. Other people and businesses catch on to what you are promoting and want a piece of the action. They may have a similar product and want to poach your distribution partners, or your distribution partners may want to make more money selling a more-expensive product since they already have the market. Or maybe, one of your employees steals your distribution partner list and tries to use it for something else.

First and foremost, ensure that you have **valid and enforceable contracts** in place. I didn't write about contract structure earlier for no reason! They serve as the backbone of what's to come.

But also focus on building and maintaining the relationships with your entire network, which should always be at the forefront of your mind throughout this journey.

3 Golden Rules

Rule 1 – Meet in person

I've talked about training and educating, but the first and easiest thing you can do is to meet them in person. Conduct phone and video calls to keep tabs, but meeting them face-to-face shows them that you value them, and they are important to your business.

Rule 2 – Open line of communication

Your network must be able to contact you with questions or even for a casual chat. An open line of communication is essential to any relationship. Since your distribution channel partners help you make money, make it a priority to be available.

Rule 3 – Support them

Provide hands-on assistance and help them sell or promote. I always go to events with my channel partners, at no cost to them. I participate in conference calls when they make large deals. Being available in this way is beneficial for both of you because a) it shows them how involved you are, b) it provides you an opportunity to have casual dialogue with them, and c) you can really get to know your channel partners from the inside out.

Keeping those three rules in mind, let's analyze the specifics within your distribution channel partners. And when I say specifics, I also mean analyzing your own attitude toward your distribution partners. I have seen companies act in many self-destructing ways. Distribution networks implode and fall apart like a house of cards when business owners start thinking they are the kings, and any partner who doesn't want to keep up can leave.

To be successful in retaining your distribution channel partners, remember the fact that you need distributors more than the distributors need you. So make sure you nurture and support your network.

Analyzing your partners

First, put together a list of every entity that operates within your distribution network – from sub-distributors to channel partners. Then, separate that list into three groups:

1. Great performers
2. Average performers
3. Bad performers

Clearly defining where these entities fit helps you identify where to focus your time and resources. The goal is to have everyone positively contribute to your business.

Evaluating the performers
1. **Great performers**

    This group is your most-loved. They are essential to your monthly income targets, so treat them as such. Let them know how well they are doing and reward them with more of your time to help them make even more money:

    - Look into special offers you can provide them where they can promote exclusively.
    - Provide them with more support staff.
    - Reward them with prizes and gifts.

This group has already proven that they believe in your business and demonstrated that faith in their sales. Not only do you benefit from the revenue they generate, but they are your best ambassadors for making your average and bad performers want more. By demonstrating their success, you motivate your other distribution channel partners to work harder.

2. **Average performers**

   This group typically makes up the majority of your network, and you need to pay a lot of attention to them. They sell with relative consistency but not in high numbers. You appreciate their work ethic, and combined, they provide most of your brand advertising in the market.

What tends to happen is that your great performers usually have such powerful access to an existing pool of prospects or buyers that they don't actually market that much. They generally have laser-focused marketing campaigns, targeting those groups directly.

Your broader advertising efforts usually come from your collective group of average performers. So, spend time showing them how much you appreciate their effort:

- Reward them with free deals that come in from clients who approach your business directly.

- Assign your own staff to work with them and help them close more deals.
- Provide them with support infrastructure and coaching.
- Set goals with rewards, which they can receive for hitting key performance indicators.

Keep your lines of communication open to them at all times, just as you do with your great performers. With the right nurturing, these average performers can grow to become your great performers, so retention is vital.

3. **Bad performers**

   You already know everyone in this group. They are the people who ghost you as soon as they sign up. Or, they are the ones who attend every webinar, call in all the time, have hundreds of questions, but never actually sell anything. They make excuses about market shifts, customer appetite, and always jump at the opportunity to complain about the competition, both externally and about other distributors snapping up all their potential customers.

   You can either forget about them, which I have done many times. Or, do something I've learned that works well. You see… even the bad performers can be useful because they are still attempting to sell. And by doing this, they continue building your brand awareness through their marketing efforts. Just because they are not bringing in any deals doesn't mean they have no value.

In the past, I successfully helped bad performers who did great with lead generation and marketing but struggled to close sales. For an agreed commission split, I partnered an average performer, who was better at closing sales but lacked available leads, to work with a bad performer, who had lots of leads but struggled to close them. It worked out great for me because I made more money, but equally, the alliance between those two partners flourished because they both earned more than before.

To keep your network working for you, it's best to really analyze them and **figure out what they need help with and offer solutions**. This keeps them embedded and producing for you.

Branding for retention

I touched on branding earlier, but it is especially important as far as retention is concerned. Just look at Apple. Create your own branding and marketing materials for your distribution channel partners to use to sell directly to their customers. They are essentially acting on behalf of your business or the business you represent.

The good news is that your distributors can be worldwide, so you benefit from the mix of marketing strategies they each use to promote your business. You'll tap into various countries in multiple languages, using whatever the most effective marketing channels are in that market.

Your business benefits immensely from the recognition and brand awareness, making it easier for your business to gain acceptance in those specific markets. Sometimes, you find that your channel partners need to rebrand or edit your promotional material to suit their requirements, relating to their own prospecting. But the product stays the same and so will most of the information.

Your priority is to increase your customer base and sell fast to make lots of money. Whereas, their priority is to sell quickly through their established network of clients and get paid quickly.

When one of my distribution channel partners is willing, I have them brand or rebrand under my umbrella business. This could be as simple as giving them an email under the guise of it being useful for closing customers, without the worry of them trying to circumvent you. This can and does happen, by the way!

By adopting your brand, they benefit from the recognition and brand awareness your entire distribution channel is helping to build, giving them a greater presence in their respective markets. So, this strategy is clearly beneficial for your distribution partner to make sales. And, it is harder for them to disengage with you or take on a different product or service since they are so heavily embedded.

Partners still being poached?

But what happens if you've followed all my advice and competitors are still poaching your distributors?

No matter how well you internally manage your distribution network, it is ultimately impossible to keep everyone happy. You will always come across channel partners who will either leave you or be poached away. If this happens consistently, however, reevaluate your business and ask yourself the following questions:

1. Are my products or services priced incorrectly?
2. Is my customer service up to standard?
3. Do we deliver on what we promise?
4. Are customers getting the products or services in a timely fashion?
5. Am I paying my distribution partners enough per sale?
6. Is the competition becoming too intrusive?
7. Is the demand for this product or service falling at the customer level?
8. Are there any legal issues your business faced that were detrimental?

Look inward first rather than blaming others. Asking yourself these tough questions helps you understand whether the issues relate to your business or something else. Look back at the way you evaluated your business and see if you missed something. We discussed the lens to look through in-depth. Revisit that section if necessary

Sometimes, you need to consider the basic fact that there are most likely other substitutes for your products or services. This could be through the end-user regarding which products or services they are willing to opt for, or you could have competitors who are competing with you on how much they pay their distribution partners.

If this is the case and you are losing distribution channel partners because they are going to work with your competition, revisit their contracts. If they are breaching contractual agreements, which you both signed, you may be able to restrict what they can do after they leave. Ideally, you do not want this to happen, but sometimes you need to take that step.

Weigh the risk-reward on whether or not to take legal action. Take time to properly analyze what or who is at fault, and figure out if there are other ways you can retain your distribution partners. Legal action can become extremely expensive, and feuds can become known to your other channel partners, which can be a negative factor. It usually is! But then again, you don't want to look like a pushover. As I said, weigh the risk-reward before you have someone served.

In closing

Now, it's time to execute! Here's your step-by-step guide.

Step 1: Prepare – Get into the right mindset and manage your expectations

By this point, we should be on the same page. Now, it's time to take your first steps. I explained that this is not a get-rich-quick program because there's work you need to put into it. If you do the work, it should be obvious by now how fast you can expect to increase sales and grow your market exposure.

Step 2: Industry Intelligence – Reduce the risk of a failed launch

Analyze your product or service to ensure the marketing features, sales collateral, and due diligence stand up to the demands of your buyer groups and potential distribution partners. Go through your DSSD Checklist (www.slicesmakealoaf.com) and make sure you've covered every angle.

Step 3: Distribution Strategy – Coordinated deployment

Design your strategy for a staged release of your product or service to distribution partners in key target markets, optimized according to your objectives, milestones, and timelines. Put your deal together, coupled with a compelling structure with a logical rationale, for true scalability. This is all about strategically positioning your product or service so that it's compelling to the prospective distribution partner.

Step 4: Marketing Collateral – Provide quality material to partners

Plan and produce your digital marketing assets, decide on multilingual translation, and provide sales scripts and tools that your partners need to sell effectively. You know your business best. Think about your copy, digital and print media, your key documents, and all your supporting information. Think about how you can make these things easily accessible in the format, medium, or language your partners require.

Step 5: Targeted Recruitment – Find the best, most capable partners

Target and penetrate your chosen markets with a combination of your search and selection of distribution partners combined with geo-targeted, sector-specific marketing to quickly build a network where it will be most effective. Look at who your competitors are working with, use social media, targeted Boolean searches, and find industry-specific introducers.

Step 6: Network Management – Relationship onboarding

Prepare to onboard both distribution partners and front-line management of all partner relationships. Plan to delegate business development to a specialist team or even an automated webinar or sales funnel working 24/7. Prepare your first contract, your agent distribution agreement, and set up systems on how you will keep track of payments made to partners when the deals start flowing in. Preparation is vital so that you can operate smoothly and demonstrate your effectiveness, management, and subsequent reliability to your partners.

Step 7: Product Training – Provide a self-paced online engagement and education program

Provide in-depth training for distribution partners to turn them into your best brand ambassadors by continuously building their interest, knowledge, confidence, and commitment through a structured education program. Plan for in-person product training as a later-phased approach and reduce costs with online tools. A good example of this would be using multimedia online education programs and learning management systems.

Step 8: Marketing Campaigns – Lead generation for partners

Assist your partners and create scalable online advertising campaigns and strategies for your top partners. Connecting them with interested clients in their target markets will help keep them embedded in your network. This will fuel their sales efforts and drive up performance across the board as your overall brand exposure is constantly growing.

Use what you have learned in this book and apply it in a way that works **for you**. Whatever has been holding you back from turning your ideas or dreams into a reality, my wish for you is to go out there and give it your all.

Throughout this book, I spoke about the lens that you need to be looking through… it's going to be a game-changer from what you've been doing. Focus on DSSD, design your deal, structure it carefully, establish scalability, and prep for distribution to achieve massive action quickly. I explained ways to achieve all this through either low-cost or no-cost strategies.

This is all about the hustle and doing what you need to do, to be who you want to become. And if you fail, then pick yourself back up and try again because persistence begets success!

If you want to dive deeper and further explore the practical implementations of my DSSD system, I highly recommend investing in the training platform that accompanies this book, which can be found at www.slicesmakealoaf.com.

DISCLAIMER: *The information in this book comes from my personal experience and knowledge. I am not a licensed legal or financial professional. I generalize this information as guidelines, which are intended to be used for information purposes only and do not constitute professional advice. Please consult independent legal and financial advice for information specific to your country, business, and circumstances. Slices Make A Loaf is not liable to you in any way for your use or reliance on my guidance or the information contained in this book or the accompanying training platform.*

Acknowledgments

This book would not have been possible without the support of my wife, the love of my life, Erika. Your love, strength, and encouragement keep me grounded through the ups and downs. To my daughter, whose sheer presence in my life gave me the inspiration to create a legacy project. To my super-efficient, quirky, and brilliant assistant, Ying, thank you for being a constant sounding board during the creation of this book and its accompanying training platform. I also know that this book wouldn't have happened without all my business and distribution partners around the world throughout these many years. This book is only as good as it is because of all the trials, tribulations, successes, and experiences we all shared building businesses and global distribution networks from nothing. And finally, to my editor, Samantha, who tirelessly organized my manuscript, which was basically a monumental brain dump on paper!

www.ingramcontent.com/pod-product-compliance
Lightning Source LLC
Chambersburg PA
CBHW052354220526
45465CB00003BA/1095